LESLIE M. BOSSERMAN

EMOTIONAL ENDURANCE

Faith-Fueled Skills for Bouncing Back

ZONDERVAN®

ZONDERVAN

Emotional Endurance

Published by Zondervan, 3950 Sparks Drive SE, Suite 101, Grand Rapids, Michigan 49546, USA. by Zondervan. Zondervan is a registered trademark of The Zondervan Corporation, L.L.C., a wholly owned subsidiary of HarperCollins Christian Publishing, Inc. Requests for information should be addressed to customercare@harpercollins.com.

ISBN 978-0-31046-744-1 (HC)
ISBN 978-0-31046-747-2 (audiobook)
ISBN 978-0-31046-746-5 (eBook)

Published in association with Books & Such Literary Management, www.booksandsuch.com.

HarperCollins Publishers, Macken House, 39/40 Mayor Street Upper, Dublin 1, D01 C9W8, Ireland (https://www.harpercollins.com)

Art direction and interior illustrations: Sabryna Lugge
Interior design: Denise Froehlich

Printed in Malaysia

26 27 28 29 30 31 PJM 10 9 8 7 6 5 4 3 2 1

For those who are weary, wandering, and wondering when it will get better, may these words provide hope for your journey and skills for your practice.

And to my best friend and husband, Joel, for building my capacity to handle what's hard while sharing in all the good. Thank you for teaching me the value of getting uncomfortable so I could grow.

CONTENTS

THE NEED FOR EMOTIONAL ENDURANCE

I am not a runner. In fact, I have often joked that I typically only run after kids and toward goals. Definitely not for recreation. And only when necessary.

But in 2007, I found myself training for a marathon.

Compelled by the mission of a nonprofit training program, I raised money for their cause while logging more than six hundred miles in six months. Training weekly with the group, I learned how to pace myself so I didn't injure my body. Slow and steady, we used a training method that followed a run-walk rhythm to stay on track as we gained mileage.

On race day I felt as ready as I'd ever be. I had stuck to my training regimen, fueled my body, and prepared my mind. Following the interval timer on my sports watch, I kept the pace as my mileage passed into double digits. When my body felt tired, my mental training kicked in. Until I reached mile twenty-two.

With less than five miles before I crossed the finish line, my legs were desperate to take an extra-long walk break. *No one will ever know*, whispered an encouraging voice in my head, which was enough for me to ignore the beeping watch telling me it was time to run again.

I continued walking and sipping electrolyte water when I heard a steady, rhythmic noise coming from behind me. In my peripheral vision, I saw a middle-aged man dressed entirely in neon, belly-down on a skateboard. As a paraplegic, he was wearing elbow guards and propelling himself forward using the sheer force of his upper-body strength.

Right then, I knew whatever I had endured to get to this place paled in comparison to this man's journey. I quickly felt my legs pick up the pace, and before I knew it, I was across the finish line.

Days later as my body recovered, I realized I could not have finished the race if I had relied on my physical strength alone. My mental focus and emotional fortitude to keep going, combined with the external motivation from witnessing the tenacity of the man on the skateboard, had pushed me forward.

My strength had prepared me for race day.

My endurance helped me finish strong.

Running a marathon had never been on my bucket list. It didn't even make the top one hundred things I hoped to do in my life. Growing up playing softball, I enjoyed the short, fast-paced sprints between bases. But the marathon training process changed me. I learned invaluable lessons about myself and what the human body is truly capable of.

I had to increase my strength in order to enhance my endurance.

Right now, each of us is already running a long race called life. And if we want to shift from *surviving* to *thriving*, we need to develop both strength *and* endurance. These concepts are often associated, and for good reason: They show up together in the best scenarios. Our strength is how much we're able to handle *before* things get hard, and our endurance is how far we can go *after* it's already hard.

Our strength is how much we're able to handle ***before*** *things get hard, and our endurance is how far we can go* ***after*** *it's already hard.*

But strength isn't just how much weight you can bench-press; it's mental too. Developing psychological strength enhances a different type of endurance—one that we are intentionally designed to cultivate throughout our lives, especially when we face setbacks that set us up for what's next.

Life isn't predictable, easy, or fun at times. We all experience moments we never planned for or uncertainty we have to navigate without a road map. Whether you're facing a new struggle or dealing with an ongoing issue, it's common to feel emotionally depleted and hopeless, especially when challenges seem too heavy to hold.

When tough stuff happens, why do some people choose to blame others, play small, or stay stuck? And why do others decide to get up, dust themselves off, and move forward? What sets apart those who allow hardship to keep them down from those who choose to rise above it?

From decades of research and practice as an educator and entrepreneur, I've identified core qualities that successful, healthy people activate as they face unexpected challenges: They are able to overcome because of *what* they learn from their experiences as well as *who* they choose to become, despite their circumstances. These resilient individuals activate a set of skills to regain emotional regulation as they learn to **cope**, **conquer** what's in their path, and **continue** on. Their inner fortitude and emotional strength empower their perseverance.

Powerful patterns emerged while I coached clients and trained teams dealing with adversity and uncertainty, from nonprofits and government agencies to start-ups and Fortune 500 companies. Their varied responses to challenges led me to dive deeper into understanding how these trends showed up across different environments: from our personal identities as individuals, partners, and parents, to our professional lives as employees, leaders, and entrepreneurs.

Studying popular leadership and business development books while researching themes like resilience and grit, I also noticed an essential component that is rarely highlighted—one we were created to cultivate and purposefully designed to develop.

Emotional endurance.

Emotional endurance *is the dynamic inner capacity to keep going and rise above our circumstances as we deal with life's stresses and challenges.*

Just as a marathon runner requires physical endurance, we need emotional endurance to persevere through life's challenges—especially when the finish line isn't in sight. But where does emotional endurance come from? Is it something you're just born with, or can you develop it throughout your life?

Emotional endurance requires a unique set of psychological skills that can be developed and activated through spiritual strength during challenging times.

Individuals who have honed their emotional endurance live with an inner fortitude that's grounded in something bigger than themselves—and that motivating *why* keeps them going. Their purpose drives their decisions and aligns their actions with their values. They resolve to do what it takes while remaining humble and flexible as they rise to the challenges in their path and continue to overcome. They learn from their mistakes and misfortunes rather than becoming absorbed by them. They use their strengths to activate their values and champion their purpose.

Understanding Our Feedback Loop

Becoming more emotionally resilient and agile helps us use our emotions to our advantage rather than letting our best intentions get hijacked by a negative reaction. Understanding our feedback loop is the starting point for developing emotional endurance.

What actually happens when we experience something unexpected or unpleasant? When a stressful event occurs, we start by feeling a specific emotion—fear, doubt, anger, surprise, sadness—that fuels related thoughts that are filtered through familiar scripts we have adopted throughout our lives.

Our emotions and thoughts shape our behaviors and performance.

We form habits over time based on consistent action that shapes our character by transforming how we *think* about our behavior. These past patterns of behavior shape our reputation, teaching others what to expect and how to treat us.

How we are received by others also impacts our emotional

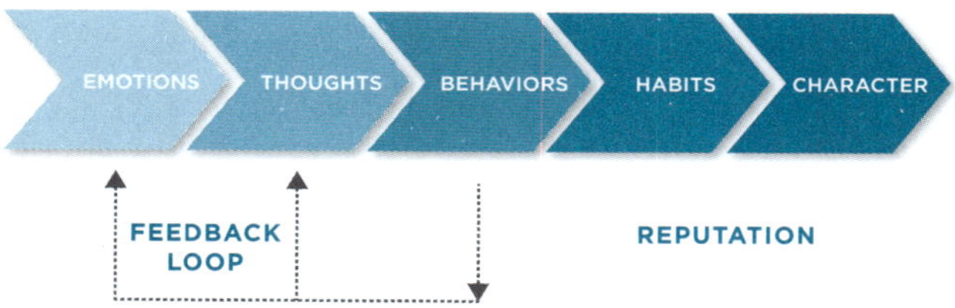

response.[1] If someone interprets our behavior in a way that wasn't intended, we take in their reaction and are able to modify future behavior. This feedback loop plays directly back to our emotions and thoughts, either fueling our unhealthy reactions or helping reframe our intentional responses.

We were intelligently designed by a thoughtful Creator who gave us the gift of free will.[2] Instead of seeing ourselves as victims of circumstance, we have agency and ability to modify how we think and what we do. As we continually overcome in the face of setbacks, we change, adapt, and grow, transforming our present suffering into perseverance as we develop our character toward a greater hope.[3]

Enhancing Emotional Endurance

Maintaining a positive outlook during times of uncertainty has been shown to have lasting impacts on our well-being, especially when coping with severe stress.[4] As we improve our mental, emotional, and psychological abilities to cope during adversity, we expand what we're able to handle in the future. This is how we grow our inner capacity for emotional endurance.

Based on our personality and background, each of us has a certain ability to deal with transitions, uncertainties, and misfortunes. Some individuals seem to have a thicker skin or a more natural bounce-back. Others must work harder to cultivate their resolve and resiliency.

While we don't have control over where our journey to developing emotional endurance begins, we can choose how to respond when we're faced with challenging circumstances. We develop emotional endurance when we are exposed to situations that are challenging enough to cause stress but manageable enough that we can learn how to cope and persevere.

Enhancing our emotional endurance expands both the range *and* the depth of how much we can handle when things get hard *and* we still choose to keep going. Instead of staying stuck or lost, we lean into uncertainty and challenges as we grow our ability to move forward with purpose.

The following six principles make up the framework for developing emotional endurance throughout your life:

1. Fortitude to Fail
2. Resilience to Rise
3. Hope to Heal
4. Courage to Change
5. Energy to Engage
6. Purpose to Persevere

Together we will explore and apply this framework to strengthen our emotional endurance through a series of intentional practices as we learn science-based skills proven by Scripture that are available to everyone—whether you're managing an organization, coaching a Little League team, or simply trying to tackle that never-ending pile of laundry!

In each section you'll explore what is already working for you now as well as consider areas you may want to modify, minimize, or manage. Reflecting on your own story and unique purpose for your life, you'll have the opportunity to integrate your faith to forge your pathway through hard times. While you try on new ways of thinking, being, and doing, you'll develop your capacity for emotional endurance.

If you told my teenage self that one day I would be an entrepreneur managing multiple businesses and married to someone I've known for over three decades (who *is* a competitive runner), she would either look at you in disbelief or give you the *biggest* high five! Through our friendship and marriage, my husband, Joel, and I have created a beautiful and dynamic life together as we live out our family motto of "Be a Blessing" in our community.

We have the privilege of parenting three diverse children, one with special needs, who is my greatest teacher. We have built and grown businesses that have supported hundreds of local families with young children while raising our own. We have applied the principles found within these pages to our own lives. While building emotional endurance hasn't been easy, we've seen how the skills shared in this book work as we continue expanding our capacity to keep going strong.

Whether you're navigating personal or professional transitions, experiencing loss and grief, or stepping into new adventures, you have the capacity to change for the better. **This book is designed to equip and empower you with biblically based skills grounded in scientific research so you can develop emotional endurance throughout your life.** If you're unsure, afraid, or maybe even *ready* to start but don't know how, I'm here to encourage you along the way as your champion for inner change. Join me as we go on a deep dive into transforming your life for an eternal purpose!

PRINCIPLE ONE

FORTITUDE TO FAIL

As we learn how to endure, we often are faced with setbacks that set us up for what's next. Experiencing failure gives us the opportunity to cultivate the **fortitude to recover and the spiritual stamina to get back up and continue.** Yet when we feel stuck in emotional quicksand, it's hard to pull ourselves out and even harder to keep going. Let's begin by learning skills for understanding, managing, and recovering from failure as we remain focused on our goals and vision for the future.

SKILL 1

NAME IT TO TAME IT

"I can't do this!" our firstborn, Caleb, screamed in exasperation as he tried to build the next part of the LEGO set. Watching his five-year-old fingers struggle to fit the small brick in the correct spot, I could clearly see his frustration growing.

Instead of swooping in to assist, I simply affirmed what I noticed. "You sound frustrated, buddy."

"I'm not frustrated. I'm disappointed!"

His strong reaction made me pause. Disappointment? That's a big emotion for a little kid!

"This shouldn't be so hard, Mom," he whimpered.

When something important to us is at stake, our emotions show up. Sometimes they're small and subtle, but often they can feel pretty strong, like Caleb's reaction. When we experience a tidal wave of emotions that are *so* intense, at first we may not even know what we're feeling. When this happens, we likely have been triggered by a hard situation or something we've avoided in the past. And all of a sudden, we find ourselves overwhelmed by difficult emotions and behave in ways that aren't so helpful.

Have you been there? I sure have!

But here's something I've learned about emotions: They're messengers, not marching orders. Just because we feel something doesn't mean we need to act on it. Our emotions share important information about what's going on around and inside us, and how those things line up with our beliefs about ourselves and our place in the world. When we understand what we're feeling and why we're feeling it, we're able to regulate our emotions and avoid getting hijacked by our triggers. When we name our emotions and accept them, we can move through their intensity.

Emotions are messengers, not marching orders.

Having the vocabulary to label our emotions is vital to developing accurate self-awareness so we can manage our feelings effectively. A recent study suggests that a minimum of twenty-seven distinct emotions interact to create a myriad of combinations that form the feelings we experience.[1] Research on emotional regulation shows that accurately naming how you're feeling can reduce the negative intensity of emotions, impacting your well-being.[2]

That's what I saw in Caleb as soon as he named *his* emotion. He was feeling triggered by his inability to put together the LEGO set the way he wanted. But once he realized exactly what he was feeling—disappointment—a wave of relief washed over his entire body. When we can name our emotions and recognize their triggers, then we can tame them.

Name Your Triggers

"Whatever you can't *be with* is what actually controls you."

The facilitator's words hung heavy in the room, like wet clothes trying to line dry during a humid, Midwestern summer. As one of the participants in a coach training program, I allowed this truth to sink in as the cacophony of Manhattan traffic five floors below began to battle the silence in the room.

Next, the facilitator instructed us to write down what we found emotionally or physically triggering: anything we tended to avoid that prevented us from connecting with others or acting with integrity. Glancing around the room, I noticed the frowns and furrowed brows of other aspiring coaches as they faced their own moments of deep discomfort. It was clear each of us had something we were struggling to overcome.

Things like . . .

- *Experiencing rejection from a loved one*
- *Dealing with uncertainty in a health diagnosis*
- *Feeling like an imposter*

But as I looked down at my own list, I noticed something shifting inside me. The discomfort I normally experienced when I thought about these things felt . . . lighter. In fact, reading the triggers written down outside of me made me feel like I was standing on top of a mountain looking down at the hard path that led to the summit. From this bird's-eye view, I could see the rocky parts of the trail to avoid if I ever came this way again. I also noticed places I could safely pause in order to catch my breath and keep climbing.

There is a powerful space between naming and owning that stretches from the point of recognition toward purposeful action. Listing my triggers was like having a trail map guiding me up the mountain that could unlock my own future success. And suddenly, when I thought about moving forward, I felt a little calmer and a lot more confident.

Now, as a seasoned executive coach with more experience, I recognize this truth: Taking a step back from a stressful situation creates some emotional distance that gives us the space to process hard moments so we can identify what's really going on under the surface. This intentional pause coupled with self-awareness increases our mental focus and psychological control.

And that comes in handy when the lies and limiting beliefs we internalize start to echo loudly in our minds.

Silence Your Saboteurs

If you're like me, you may have a nagging inner voice that repeats a familiar script:

- *You're not good enough.*
- *No one will choose you.*
- *You're not worthy of being loved.*

- *Who do you think you really are?*
- *You're such a failure.*

Sound familiar?

Maybe the voice sounds like a person from your childhood: someone who was supposed to care for and champion you but instead fed you these lies. Or perhaps these limiting beliefs are repeated in your *own* voice—silent or spoken—until they have become the default scripts your mind plays on repeat.

These voices that tear you down instead of building you up? They're your *Saboteurs*: the thought gremlins that ambush you when you're dealing with your most challenging circumstances.

Our Saboteurs are generally the personifications of our fears, regrets, self-doubts, frustrations, and anxieties. And they sabotage us by feeding off our insecurities and shining a spotlight on our failures. They activate a feedback loop of negativity that hijacks our performance at work, our relationships with others, and our overall well-being.

Yet there was a time when most of us didn't have these Saboteurs in our lives. So where do they come from? While children are naturally curious, full of wonder, and extremely resilient, they soon learn to follow rules created to keep them safe. Most Saboteurs first emerge in childhood not to harm us but to protect us.

Curious children grow into cautious adults who remember what it was like when they were scolded or felt embarrassed or ashamed. Those painful memories compel us to choose *not* to try, *not* to risk, *not* to go after things that don't have known outcomes and safe boundaries. As adults, if we don't push past those memories and refuse to challenge ourselves, we learn to play small, risk less, and pass on opportunities.

So what happens when we don't silence these Saboteurs?

Over time, they shape our neural pathways, coding how we think, feel, behave, and interact with others. Then when we face a stressful situation, our Saboteurs steal our focus and feed us lies that we have accepted as familiar truths.

Talk about a depressing feedback loop, right? But here's the good news:

We don't have to stay chained to our Saboteurs or our triggers.

Like 2 Corinthians 10:5 reminds us, we can "take captive every thought to make it obedient to Christ" (NIV). That's a promise I've found helpful time and again. I'll show you why and what you can do to silence your Saboteurs.

Tame Your Triggers with Truth

Now it's your turn to consider your triggers as we try an easy exercise together. Take a moment to name people, situations, or emotions you can't *be with*. Write down as many relationships and circumstances as you can—both internal and external—that really get under your skin. Here are a few of my own to get you started:

- *Distracted drivers on their phones*

- *When sock orphans emerge from the laundry (after two went in!)*
- *People who don't clean up after their pets or children*
- *Adults who play the victim instead of taking ownership of their choices*

So what sets *you* off? And—here's the kicker—how do you react in these moments? Are you proud of your response, or does your behavior take you further away from the person you want to be?

Grab a notebook and pen, and take a few minutes to capture whatever is top of mind and feels too hard or heavy for you to hold.

Now, here's the next part of the exercise: Recall that harsh inner voice and the negative things it repeats. Do those things add up to who God says you are? If not, then congratulations—you've identified the lies your Saboteurs have been feeding you! You're one step closer to breaking away from the negative emotions keeping you stuck.

Once you have listed your triggers and your Saboteurs' lies, it's time to reframe them with the truth of what God says about you. Let's try this together using one of the biggest lies I believed for over two decades.

LIE: *You are not enough, no matter how hard you try or what you accomplish.*

TRUTH: *You are enough as a beloved child of God, who has made you in His image for a purpose.*[3]

You also have access to this truth.

You don't have to stay stuck in the spiral of your negative emotions. When you name what you're feeling, recognize and manage your triggers, and replace your Saboteurs' lies with truth, you can move through the swell of your emotions. And when you choose to focus on what is true, righteous, holy, and good, the lies no longer have a stronghold on your mind.[4]

It's important to note that we were never meant to approve of or *be with* the immoral, the profane, and the ungodly things of this world that corrupt and pollute. The apostle Paul addressed the Romans, who were living in the middle of a society twisted by perverse behaviors, and encouraged them to live a set-apart life: "Do not be conformed to this age, but be transformed by the renewing of the mind, so that you may discern what is the will of God—what is good and acceptable and perfect" (Romans 12:2 NRSVue).

We are to focus on heavenly things while living this earthly life. We're not supposed to accept everything or *be with* what is evil but rather choose to overcome evil with what is good. By recognizing our emotions and naming the lies our Saboteurs are broadcasting, we can tame our triggers and overcome with emotional endurance.

REFLECT + CONNECT

Identify one emotional trigger that has been sabotaging your progress toward achieving your goals and track its pattern for one week.

- When and where does this trigger show up?
- In a moment when you're feeling triggered, try this: Slow down, name what you're feeling, and then track your emotions for the next fifteen minutes. How did naming your emotions change your response?
- When your Saboteur begins whispering negative words, what truths from Scripture can you turn to as you make new things possible?

SKILL 2

LEARN TO DISCERN

I still remember how it felt sitting behind the anchor desk for the first time on the *Bruin News 29* station set, eager and ready. As a bright-eyed eighteen-year-old, I had moved to Los Angeles to pursue a career in broadcast journalism. On campus, I started out as a beat reporter for our student station before I moved up and became a producer, then finally achieved the coveted role of evening anchor.

As the green light flashed "on air" and the teleprompter started to roll, I began the evening news update: a human-interest story about a student-initiated program to provide water bottles and blankets to the local homeless population. Hundreds of students showed up to serve and make a difference. As I read the closing line, I watched the light switch back from green to red, signaling the end of the broadcast.

While my anchor duties were done for the night, the story stayed with me as I made my way back to my dorm room. I lived on campus and was active in my residence hall community, so why hadn't I heard about this service project *before* it happened? A nagging sense of unease kept a powerful thought scrolling through my mind: *If I want to make a difference and do work that matters, I need to be the one making the change happen, not reporting on it after it occurs.*

That was when I realized I was on the *wrong* side of the camera.

Defining moments often happen when we least expect them. We can be going through the everyday motions of our lives when, all of a sudden, something challenges the way we look at our world, our loved ones, or even ourselves. If you've experienced a defining moment that's changed the trajectory of your life, you likely recognized when something inside you began to shift—and you've never been the same since.

That's how I felt sitting in my dorm room that night. Everything I thought I wanted to pursue, study, and achieve was in question. Moments before, my career path felt known and paved. Suddenly my future was uncertain, without a road map forward.

Stop While You're Behind

I'm sure you've heard the phrase "quit while you're ahead." People say it when they've hit success but fear their luck will eventually run out. So they figure it's better to stop where they are and be content with whatever they've earned instead of moving forward and risking a loss.

But what happens when you haven't reached success yet? When, instead, you feel *behind* with no clear path forward? This was the place I found myself in over twenty years ago after my first on-air broadcast. Behind and very, very lost.

What would I do now? Where would I go from here?

The first time I began to make progress toward a new path was when I learned how to be comfortable with being uncomfortable. I stopped while I felt behind so I could move forward in the right direction, starting with learning how to discern.

While reading the formative book *Let Your Life Speak*, one line the author and educator, Parker Palmer, wrote stopped me in my tracks: "Vocation does not come from willfulness. It comes from listening. I must listen to my life and try to understand what it is truly about—quite apart from what I would like it to be about."[1]

I can't say I relished this advice at first. Pausing to listen to my life wasn't exactly in my Type A vocabulary. As a natural planner, I found so much comfort in knowing the steps I needed to take to achieve whatever goal I set my mind to. But now I didn't have a to-do list to guide my steps. It was just me, God, and the present moment.

So I sat in my dorm room, praying for clear direction and for

God to guide my life with purpose. Normally when I had faced this kind of murkiness, I would've tried to claw back the control I had seemed to lose. I would have immediately changed my major and thrown myself into that new trajectory, hoping to find comfort in a set path forward. Instead, I leaned into the uncertainty I felt deep in my heart as I trusted God to make a way.[2]

Choosing to surrender your future to God while sitting in the discomfort of the unknown requires faith and patience. "Surrender is the only pathway to peace, joy, and transformation," agrees author Cleere Cherry Reaves.[3] This is the golden thread that has run through my life story, even if I didn't recognize it back in college. Through teaching me how to trust and surrender, God was shifting and shaping my life for His bigger plan and purpose by growing my ability to face the unknown with fortitude rather than focusing on failure.

Reflect Softer

Change of any kind is hard—but especially a change you're not expecting. When my career plans bottomed out, my body's first reaction was to flood my brain with feelings of stress and worry: *Now what? How do I move forward? Can I even move forward if I don't know where I'm going? I'm not equipped for this! What's next?* But have you ever stopped to consider that what you might be doing five or ten years into your future may not have been invented yet, or the need realized? From the creation of the wheel and electricity to more modern inventions like the internet, artificial intelligence, and solar power, innovation opens new opportunities that may not even seem possible now.

When you're on a path where the way forward is unclear or your gut is telling you *this isn't working well*, you don't have to try harder. You can reflect softer. By staying present with your experience, even when you feel uncomfortable, you adopt a gentler approach in times of stress and uncertainty. Here, you extend yourself the grace of stopping right where you are instead of pressing on.

You don't have to try harder. You can reflect softer.

It's tempting to act quickly and make a decision, isn't it? But science shows that slowing down and taking a purposeful pause increases discernment. Behavioral economists have studied how we make decisions and discovered how two systems in our brains work together to interpret information we receive: the *emotional mind* and the *conscious mind*.[4]

The emotional mind leans into intuition to make quick decisions, while the conscious mind steps in more deliberately to evaluate, monitor, and analyze the options.[5] Discernment requires both these systems to engage so the intuitive process informs the rational mind, shaping behavior and influencing related judgments. But what happens when we have lots of different options to choose from? How do our brains decide which path is right for us? You start by getting present with what you're experiencing right now.

Take Your "Now" Step

When you're facing the future, you can learn to discern in the present. I've found that "paralysis by analysis" ends by answering one simple question: *What's* **now** *for me?* When you ask this question, what you're really doing is checking in with yourself to assess what you need right now. And discerning *what's now* becomes a compass to help you reflect as you pray daily for direction, understanding, and guidance.[6]

In my early college years, I started asking simple questions to discern my *now step* before trying to figure out the next step:

- *Is it time to study or time to play?*
- *Time to eat or time to exercise?*
- *Time to create or time to rest?*

By learning how to slow down and be gentler with myself, I was able to face my future with more faith and focus. In the midst of uncertainty, I leaned into the wisdom of Ecclesiastes 3, believing there was a time for everything that needed to be done, while leaving the rest for a later season. Rather than strive, here I learned how to listen, discern, and abide.

So if you're feeling a little lost on your path, you can learn to discern by pausing and asking yourself, *What's "now" for me?* Your answer might be the best way to move forward. Instead of focusing on your fears, doubts, and failures, this powerfully simple question invites you to realign with your present experience, trusting in God's provision as you approach decision-making with faith and integrity. Learning how to reflect with this softer approach shows how stopping is strategic for discerning your "now steps" forward. When you make the time and space for purposeful pauses in the middle of uncertain situations, you strengthen your emotional muscles of discernment.

REFLECT + CONNECT

Think back to a time when the future felt fuzzy, or reflect on a present situation that is uncertain or challenging. Then use the guiding questions below to increase your discernment:

- Notice how this experience changed the way you saw yourself or your life. How did you react to that change? In hindsight, how do you *wish* you had responded?
- How would a "reflect softer" approach help you here?
- Take a few minutes to reflect on what's *now* for you. What opportunities are present that you didn't see before?

SKILL 3

FAIL FORWARD IN YOUR STRENGTHS

I followed my new supervisor into her office as she gently shut the door behind us and motioned for me to have a seat. One month prior, I had uprooted my life on the West Coast and moved to central Illinois to start a new chapter. After finishing graduate school, I was ready for change—even if my naturally curly hair wasn't prepared for Midwest humidity!

Working in student leadership development at the University of Illinois, my days were filled with many of my favorite things: planning large-scale programs, connecting with campus partners, and cultivating relationships with alumni stakeholders. Just weeks into this new role, I was already serving on some high-profile campus committees and felt like my work was making an impact.

"Leslie, we love having you on our team," my supervisor began. "And your energy and enthusiasm are refreshing."

Pausing, she held my gaze with intention. "So I'm going to give you a piece of advice that was shared with me as a young professional that I hope you take to heart."

She went on to describe how she had felt nervous and unsure of herself when she started her first job on campus. In staff meetings, she often struggled to share her input or provide feedback. Instead of speaking up, she shrank back, trying to blend in and become invisible.

"Then one day, my boss pulled me aside and said, 'All you have to do is say *one good thing* in each meeting,' and it became my personal challenge. Each time I spoke up, my confidence grew stronger until I found my voice."

I listened with curiosity as someone I viewed as a poised professional shared such a vulnerable and powerful memory. But I was missing the story's connection to my own career path. As a natural extrovert, I was *not* timid and had no problem speaking up!

My supervisor smiled kindly, meeting my gaze, and continued. "I'm going to share the same advice with you now but for the exact *opposite* reason: When you're in a meeting, say *just* one good thing. You don't need to share all your thoughts and ideas. Give others a chance to get to know you and trust your abilities without making it appear like you have all the answers."

I paused, taking in what she had shared.

Did she just call me a know-it-all?

I was crushed! My enthusiasm and excitement had backfired, and my new supervisor had noticed. By oversharing my ideas, I hadn't left space for others to contribute, unintentionally silencing colleagues who otherwise might have participated. The truth hit hard. How could I have let my passion get so carried away? Would I be able to tone it down in the future while still acting like myself? Feeling equal parts shocked, humbled, and grateful for the insight and advice, I knew I had to learn how to moderate my enthusiasm.

This unintentional error early in my career taught me a valuable lesson: Your strengths aren't always going to be effective in every situation. Sometimes you won't use them appropriately, or sometimes you'll fall short, even when those same strengths have gotten you where you are now.

Even still, **it's possible to recognize and regulate your strengths**. When you learn to apply your strengths in the right context and amount, you can mitigate potential failure—especially in areas where you have natural talent.

And as you learn how to prepare for *and* recover from failure, you build more emotional endurance.

Consider the Context

Our Creator designed us with the aptitude for using our strengths for good in service to others.[1] Yet, as I learned as a young professional, without guidelines, our best efforts may unintentionally backfire. You also may have felt the shock and disappointment of relying on strengths that, for one reason or another, didn't deliver. In fact, the sting of failing in an area of strength often feels harsher than facing failure in an area of weakness.

As you learn how to prepare for and *recover from failure, you build more emotional endurance.*

Strengths are naturally energizing, *dynamic potentials* that can be modified and applied based on the situation and regulated accordingly. They are complex and variable in nature, shifting based on the needs and demands of the specific environment. Like choosing the perfect playlist or adjusting the lighting to match the mood, we regulate our strengths based on the situation: Using the right **strength**, in the right **amount**, in the right **way**, at the right **time** is key.[2]

Strengths are naturally energizing,* dynamic potentials *that can be modified and applied based on the situation and regulated accordingly.

For example, let's say you decide to go skydiving. You'll likely do your research to find a qualified instructor and then check to make sure you have a functional parachute before you jump. While a parachute is designed to provide a safe landing when you fall from a high altitude out of an airplane, this same tool would do little good if you chose to jump off the roof of your house. There's not enough time to activate a parachute at that low altitude!

Our failures are often the result of over- or under-using our natural strengths out of context. It's not enough to know what we're good at and simply do it more often. We need to understand the environment and energy yield so we can effectively regulate and activate our strengths. You have to consider the context when you use your strengths to achieve success. Sometimes you need a parachute. Other times, you need a very large trampoline to break your fall. And when you misjudge the situation, learning how to bounce back and recover is what enhances your emotional endurance. Here, failure becomes a powerful teacher.

Learn to Fail

We all reach a point when we realize the strengths we've developed just aren't working for the situation at hand. Or maybe the situation calls for something different, yet we keep doing what's familiar. Instead of using our strengths more, we can proactively prepare for *failure* in order to develop emotional endurance for the long haul.

I can guess what you're thinking: *Wait, did Leslie just tell me I need to learn to fail?* Yes, but not in the way you may have thought about failure before. Here are three strategies to face failure with fortitude that have helped me tremendously:

1. **Intentionally Plan to Fail:** If we assume that success has a specific formula and that hard work always produces positive results, we set ourselves up for a lifetime of disappointment. Sometimes our best effort isn't enough for the situation we're in. Since experiencing failure is inevitable, we need to plan for it. If we proactively consider what failure looks and feels like, we will be better able to recognize and recover from it when it happens. Plan for failure now by thinking through these questions:

- Think back to a time when—despite working from your strengths—the outcome didn't go as planned. How did you feel? What did you do?
- Consider what you wish you had known or done differently. How can this insight change your future response to failure?
- Now make a very specific plan for how you're going to treat yourself and others the next time you experience failure. What will you do and not do?
- When we plan ahead for how we will respond in the face of failure, we bounce back faster.

2. **Evaluate the Environment:** Once you have your plan in place, take a moment to notice which of your strengths might help forge a new way forward in the situation you're facing.
   - What opportunities are possible based on the resources that are available to you?
   - What do you need to be mindful to avoid?
   - How can you regulate your strengths to reach your desired outcome?

Consider if there's a strength you need but do not have that might help this particular situation. Then think of a friend or colleague who has this strength and ask them for support.

3. **Reboot and Recover:** When you face failure, remind yourself that you already have a plan in place for

this exact moment—and follow it! While it's often tempting to retreat or make excuses, commit to staying present in the moment as you learn from your experience by asking yourself:

- How am I feeling now?
- What can this situation teach me?
- What do I need most moving forward?

By accepting that you're still learning and becoming better, you will be able to activate your inner strength to keep going. And remember this: You're never doing it alone.[3]

Through the words of the apostle James, we can see how to align our attitudes whenever we face challenges: "Consider it pure joy, my brothers and sisters, whenever you face trials of many kinds, because you know that the testing of your faith produces perseverance. Let perseverance finish its work so that you may be mature and complete, not lacking anything" (James 1:2–4 NIV).

What if we allowed our character to be tested so it could be perfected? This is exactly God's plan for us as we journey through our physical life. Consider how much others learn when they watch us grow through—and because of—our failures. When we aren't successful, God's true strength is magnified in the absence of our own.[4] Here, failure becomes the foundation to receive a greater gift.

Facing hardship helps you develop perseverance. And *perseverance* is a core building block for developing your *emotional endurance*. Our strength doesn't begin or end with us.[5] When our own strengths fall short, we can lean on God's eternal strength. And in doing so, we're built back up as we fail forward and bounce back with greater perseverance to face whatever comes next.

REFLECT + CONNECT

Use these questions as you reflect on your strengths and create a plan for facing failure when it occurs:

- What are you top three strengths? Think of areas that bring you energy and joy while producing exceptional results.
- Now consider a time when you over- or under-applied one of your strengths. What was the result? What did you learn from this situation?
- Make a plan to face future failure. How will you reboot and recover?

PRINCIPLE TWO

RESILIENCE TO RISE

Once we understand how to define and plan for failure, we must also learn how to **exercise resilience to rise and continue on**, especially when the path forward isn't clear. From seasons when we feel stuck or stalled out to simply not knowing which option to choose, persevering with purpose allows us to move from our *now step* so we can take our next step. Together, let's dive deeper to understand our responses to uncertainty and the true source of our identity in Christ as we rise up with emotional endurance.

SKILL 4

FACE THE UNKNOWN WITH FAITH

One phone call changed my life.

Staring at the glowing screen, I was at a mental crossroads, deciding whether to answer or just let the call go to voicemail. Did I even have the energy? My finger hovered over the phone screen as I wrestled with what to do. Silently praying, I tapped the green circle and softly said, "Hi."

The voice on the other end was familiar, warm, and welcoming. "Leslie! How are you doing?" As one of my oldest and closest friends, the caller was someone as safe and comfortable as the blanket wrapped around my weary body.

"I've been better." The floodgate of tears I had been carefully holding at bay finally broke. Letting them wash over me, I took in a long, deep breath and dove into what I'd recently been through.

From the outside looking in, my life appeared nearly perfect. But my body felt broken.

What began as fatigue had grown into a chronic illness I couldn't recover from. For weeks I had been extremely sick without a clear path for recovery. Western doctors couldn't diagnose me. Alternative medicine kept me on a regular regimen of herbal remedies, acupuncture, and rest. Still, my body refused to heal.

One particularly hard day, I struggled to get off my red couch as the rain fell relentlessly outside. I was curled into a human blanket burrito with little motivation, tired of being tired, and ready for change. My attention landed on a small book across the room, and I started reading: "And Jabez called on the God of Israel saying, 'Oh, that You would bless me indeed, and enlarge my territory, that Your hand would be with me, and that You would keep me from evil, that I may not cause pain!' So God granted him what he requested" (1 Chronicles 4:10 NKJV).

The words hit me hard in a soft place.

I realized that until then, I hadn't been praying with the same confidence and fervor Jabez exemplified in this single, powerful verse. Sure, I had asked God to heal me and help guide my life. But to *really* pray to be blessed and to have my metaphorical territory enlarged felt like *way too much.*

But what if it wasn't?

What if, instead, it was exactly what my life needed and required in that season?

How many times do we avoid asking for what we want because we are unsure, feel underqualified, or are just too afraid? That was my story for nearly three decades.

We limit ourselves by what we don't ask for.

I had to choose to continue to show up in the middle of my messy life, especially when it wasn't easy or comfortable. I had to embody the courage to pray like Jabez while remaining open to whatever the outcome would be. I had to allow myself the space and grace to grow, change, and embrace the unknown.

I had to develop emotional endurance and find the resilience to rise.

That day, something shifted in me as I poured out my heart to our Creator. I asked to be moved into the spaces and places where the talents He gave me could be used and cultivated. I asked to be kept from harm so my work and life would be filled with purpose and productivity. I asked for my path to be made known so I could find a way forward.

I asked . . . and God listened.

What happened next could only be described as divine intervention. God showed up in ways I never could have expected, and in some ways I downright didn't appreciate at the time. All for my healing and for His glory.

In a matter of weeks, my body made a remarkable recovery, and I decided to become an entrepreneur and start my coaching practice. But do you want to know the best part of my healing journey? The part that I *never* could have predicted or even master-planned?

We limit ourselves by what we don't ask for.

Less than six months after that pivotal phone call, the same friend who encouraged me to get off my red couch stood beside me in a white suit as we vowed to spend the rest of our lives together. My best friend was now also my husband. And over a decade later, we haven't stopped talking about all the incredible ways God uses our brokenness to teach us how to rise up and keep going.

Face the Brick Wall

When we are stuck in the present without a clear path forward, we often feel like we're standing in front of a solid brick wall we cannot scale. Some of us simply stand there and stare at the wall, considering all our options while not moving. Others try to beat it down, pounding the bricks until we're left with bloody knuckles and feelings of defeat. And some decide to lean against the wall, hoping someone else will come along with a solution.

Dealing with an unknown future or a frustrating present challenge often feels like standing nose-to-nose with this brick wall. We get so focused on what's right in front of us—unchanging and immovable—that we don't look for other possibilities and solutions. Few of us step back and look up, finally realizing that the wall is just above our heads and only six feet high and six feet wide. With enough space and perspective, we can simply walk around it. But we have to step back to let our egos (and our knuckles) heal first.

- *What's blocking your path forward?*
- *What are you so focused on beating down?*
- *What's preventing you from stepping back?*

Science shows how our minds and bodies experience a specific self-preserving response when faced with a stressful or unexpected circumstance. We were designed to narrow our attentional focus for survival during times of heightened negative stimulus.[1] If we feel like our physical safety is at stake, the number of available choices shrinks so we can easily make a split-second decision. This acute-stress response commonly known as "fight or flight" is a physiological state during which our bodies release hormones like adrenaline and cortisol, activating the sympathetic nervous system.[2] Then we are ready either to stay and face the issue head-on or flee.

The encouraging truth is that we can learn how to handle these challenging moments. Using a few practical tools to navigate our negative feelings and automatic responses, we can embrace and face whatever is in our path or blocking it.

Redefine Resilience

There are seasons in life when we desire more yet cannot begin to imagine what the future holds, and others that bring us to unexpected places and new territory. But what sets apart those who embrace challenges as new adventures from those who stay curled up on the couch?

While there are many ways to conceptualize resilience, the American Psychological Association defines it as "the process and outcome of successfully adapting to difficult or challenging life experiences, especially through mental, emotional, and behavioral flexibility and adjustment to external and internal demands."[3] Known for its bounce-back quality, especially in times of stress and challenge, resilience is a learned capacity of traits and environmental factors that allows us to remain flexible and adaptable instead of staying stuck.

Resilience includes both the ability to face difficulty in the present and to adaptatively respond as we build more capacity for the future. Psychologist and resilience expert Zelana Montminy advocates that resilient people don't let their adversity *define* them. Emphasizing the importance of choosing to remain flexible—both mentally and emotionally agile—she shares that "at its core, resilience is about being capable and strong enough to persevere in adverse or stressful conditions—and to take away positive meaning from that experience."[4]

Resilience includes both the ability to face difficulty in the present and to adaptatively respond as we build more capacity for the future.

Resilient people are able to adapt to change while still making choices that reinforce goals and integrity.

Positive psychologists have identified the following three factors that are essential to exercising resilience:

1. **Recovery:** Returning to a normal degree of functioning
2. **Resistance:** Experiencing limited or no signs of disturbance
3. **Reconfiguration:** Finding new stability in changing circumstances[5]

Since we were designed to overcome for an eternal purpose, we see how these three areas take on an even deeper meaning when applied to Scripture:

1. **Recovery:** "And after you have suffered a little while, the God of all grace, who has called you to his eternal glory in Christ, will himself restore, confirm, strengthen, and establish you" (1 Peter 5:10 ESV).
2. **Resistance:** "We are hard-pressed on every side, yet not crushed; we are perplexed, but not in despair; persecuted, but not forsaken; struck down, but not destroyed" (2 Corinthians 4:8–9 NKJV).
3. **Reconfiguration:** "We also glory in our sufferings, because we know that suffering produces perseverance; perseverance, character; and character, hope" (Romans 5:3–4 NIV).

We should not be surprised when we face trials and experience unwarranted persecution, because we live in a broken world.[6] Jesus Himself prepared us for this and shared how we would be asked to give up much.[7] Then He became the ultimate sacrifice so we can live with more freedom, grace, and abundance.[8]

When we face the unknown and must find a way forward, the spiritual promise that a greater reward is waiting helps refuel our hearts and minds as we exercise resilience with purpose.[9] While the scientific research on resilience is compelling, it's this larger, eternal vision for *why* we are developing emotional endurance that helps us rise up and overcome.

REFLECT + CONNECT

Identify one current challenge or uncertain area in your life that feels heavy and hard. Then apply the following resilience framework to increase your emotional endurance:

- **Recovery:** When is this issue not as bad? Notice the times you can return to your baseline.
- **Resistance:** What is one thing that makes this situation just a little bit better? Consider what shifts when the emotional friction lessens.
- **Reconfiguration:** How can you stay grounded, stable, and strong? Make a commitment to what boundaries you may need to set and remain accountable to.

SKILL 5

SHIFT YOUR PERSPECTIVE

Walking through the ornate hallways of Mysuru Palace in Southern India, I was like a child experiencing wonder for the first time. After spending the previous six months volunteering at a local school in the Middle East, I was invited to travel with the students to attend an international leadership conference in Bengaluru (Bangalore). Which was how I found myself inside a historic East Asian palace, chaperoning a group of middle school girls.

"Would your students like to see our famous stuffed animal room?" the tour guide kindly asked. "It is the most elaborate collection in all of India," she added with pride.

Knowing how much the girls loved their stuffed toys—and even brought them along while away from home—I nodded enthusiastically. *They will love this!* I thought as I followed the guide to a large hidden door in the wall.

Turning to me, the guide gestured to come close and whispered, "This space is private and not on our regular tour. We'll go in with the lights off, so let the girls know to walk carefully and stay together." Then she paused at the door and slyly smiled. "The maharaja also called this his trophy room."

I was trying to make sense of this new information as the guide quickly ushered us into a large, dark hallway. The girls giggled with anticipation until lights flooded the room. Their levity was quickly replaced with shocked silence—then sobs and wails of terror.

What I had assumed would be a historic collection of royal toys turned out to be the largest display of taxidermy I had ever seen!

Sometimes the assumptions we make based on partial information turn out to be exactly the opposite of what we thought. Comforting my young students as I politely asked to leave the room, I knew this lesson on perspective would stay with me for life. Along with the gleaming eyes of the largest stuffed tiger I had ever seen.

Look Through Different Eyes

Perspective is powerful. It shapes how we view the world based on our background, culture, past experiences, present circumstances, and future expectations. It has often been said that *perception becomes reality*. Just like my experience inside the stuffed animal room, we all have moments when things are not what we presumed. It is often easier to hold to our assumptions than engage with the emotional friction that comes when our version of reality is challenged. What if these moments invite us to look at the situation with different eyes?

One night before bed, I was reading out loud to our children from one of my favorite books, *The Phantom Tollbooth*. In the story, one of the main characters, Milo, encounters a peculiar boy named Alec, who, instead of growing vertically taller from the ground up, grows from the sky down. In a playful interchange, Alec explains, "You certainly can't always look at things from someone else's point of view. For instance, from here that looks like a bucket of water," Alec said, pointing to a nearby bucket. "But from an ant's point of view it's a vast ocean, from an elephant's just a cool drink, and to a fish, of course, it's home. So, you see, the way you see things depends a great deal on where you look at them from."[1]

This whimsical bedtime story taught us all a valuable lesson that evening: There is never only one way to look at something.

There is never only one way to look at something.

Depending on where you're standing, there are multiple vantage points to every experience. Each of us has the power to consciously choose to look through different eyes as we build empathy and grow our emotional endurance.

Shift How You See

Curious about changing your perspective? Here's a simple exercise I often use when leading organizational trainings. You'll need a blank sheet of paper, something to write with, and a timer.

1. Set your timer for thirty seconds and hit *start*.
2. Write down everything you see that is blue until the timer is done.
3. Count how many blue items you recorded.
4. Now reset the timer for thirty seconds, start it again, and *close your eyes*.
5. With your eyes closed, mentally list everything in your immediate vicinity that is red (no peeking!).
6. When the timer is done, open your eyes and count how many red items you listed compared to the blue list.

What do you notice? Over the years of doing this exercise in various groups, most people are able to list about half as many red items compared to blue items. Why is this? What makes shifting our focus to red so much harder?

In the early 1990s, psychologists Arien Mack and Irvin Rock conducted a series of perception and attention experiments where they studied "inattentional blindness": the failure to notice a fully visible but unexpected object because attention was engaged on another task, event, or object.[2] We miss the red objects in the exercise above because we're focused on counting

We tend to see whatever we are looking for, while filtering out the rest.

everything that's blue. We tend to see whatever we are looking for, while filtering out the rest.

Similar to the biological fight-or-flight response, this type of selective attention allows us to increase our productivity by dismissing what isn't necessary in the moment as our attention narrows. But did you know when we specifically experience positive emotions, the exact *opposite* occurs?

Broaden and Build Your Positive Emotions

Have you ever experienced something so wonderful that the positive feelings you have seem to fuel your energy and fill you up? Nurturing positive feelings leads to new possibilities. Instead of the limiting response of fight-or-flight, you increase your capacity for *more* positive emotions, and that broadens your thought-action repertoires and builds up an *enduring resource* you can draw on when facing future struggles.[3] This is the beginning of a beautiful feedback loop: Research conducted by positive psychologist Barbara Fredrickson shows that positive emotions increase the range of opportunities and possible behaviors, fueling psychological resiliency.[4]

Nurturing positive feelings leads to new possibilities.

The amplifying power of positive emotions helps develop our capacity to rise up in the face of hardship, increasing our emotional endurance. We are transformed, becoming more creative, knowledgeable, resilient, socially integrated, and healthy.

Scripture also has a lot to say about how our thoughts impact our emotions and overall mindset:

- **Psalm 19:14:** "Let the words of my mouth and the meditation of my heart be acceptable in your sight, O Lord, my rock and my redeemer" (ESV).
- **Proverbs 17:22:** "A joyful heart is good medicine, but a crushed spirit dries up the bones" (ESV).
- **Philippians 4:6–7:** "Do not be anxious about anything, but in everything by prayer and supplication with thanksgiving let your requests be made known to God. And the peace of God, which surpasses all understanding, will guard your hearts and your minds in Christ Jesus" (ESV).

When we focus on what causes worry and anxiety, we stay stuck. But when we shift our mindset to focus on the Spirit, we get unstuck by accessing the hope of God that renews our strength.[5] Returning to these positive emotions again and again builds emotional endurance, helping us bounce back quickly from challenges.

Choose to Become Curious

We've learned about the many benefits of positive emotions from both science and Scripture, but what if we still lack the motivation to move? What can we do when it's not as simple as stepping away from the brick wall? How can we find more resilience to rise?

Imagine what would happen if you viewed triggering times as invitations to practice curiosity.

Consider this common scenario: Someone does something you don't understand (or even agree with) and you react like this: *Why did you do that?* This accusatory *why* question tends to put the other person on the defense, triggering the automatic fight-or-flight response.

Now consider the difference if you simply shift the question so it becomes more curious and less critical: *What motivated you to do that?* Here, you are still seeking information but from a perspective that gives the other person space to share their story without feeling defensive.

Curiosity is the antidote to criticism. Choosing to *get curious* instead of critical invites a spirit of resilience to the conversation and creates more possibilities for connection. Shifting how you ask—from *why* to *what*—opens up dialogue instead of shutting it down. The motivation behind these questions allows us, and others, to rise up rather than shrink back. As we reflect on challenging situations with a curious mindset, we can ask questions like these:

Curiosity is the antidote to criticism.

- *How can I look at this situation differently?*
- *What opportunities are present?*
- *Who can I connect with for support?*
- *What is this season teaching me now?*

Throughout biblical history, individuals were encouraged to be creative and curious with appropriate direction and wisdom.

- As a young boy, David combined his curiosity with courage and chose five smooth stones and the fear of the Lord as his weapons of choice to slay Goliath.[6]
- Abagail noticed the needs of David and his mighty men and went out to meet them, saving her household and gaining a righteous husband.[7]
- Thousands came to witness Jesus, especially after hearing He raised Lazarus from the dead.[8]

Staying curious in a godly way allows us to expand what we can handle with spiritual support so we can continue to rise up and overcome.

Staying curious in a godly way allows us to expand what we can handle with spiritual support so we can continue to rise up and overcome. Over time, when we seek out information with curiosity, we can prevent our feelings from hijacking our thoughts and behaviors. As a result, we regain control over how our behavior shapes our character and reputation—*who* we are and *what* we are known for.

We get off the couch and access more curiosity.
We step away from the brick wall and find a new path forward.
We rise up and continue moving forward with resilience.

REFLECT + CONNECT

Reflecting on a recent hardship or current struggle, consider the perspective you are viewing the situation through now.

- Choose a label that fits your feelings. What words, phrases, and emotions are present?
- Next, reframe the label you chose above with a new perspective that serves you better. Try choosing a word that is positive and maybe even the opposite of your current emotional state.
- Now try on curiosity and see what shifts. What is possible because of your curiosity that you couldn't access before?

SKILL 6

CLARIFY YOUR CORE DRIVERS

Her face shone with eager anticipation as she sat across from me in the downtown café. After I had been recognized as one of Sacramento's "40 Under 40" honorees, I was meeting with one of the most influential women in our capital region. It was a pinch-me moment in my professional life!

"I have an incredible opportunity for you," she began. "Our board of directors would like to offer you a position on our leadership team. It's right up your alley with all you're doing for early childhood education and community development."

I looked back at her enthusiastic face with a mixture of raw emotion. A decade ago, I could only have dreamed of this opportunity. Yet her offer wasn't framed as a question or really even an invitation. Rather, it was an assumption that I would commit to volunteering many evenings and weekends for their cause, away from my family.

While I felt honored and humbled to be asked, the position wasn't something I was able to wholeheartedly pursue in that season of life. We were in the thick of parenting three young children—one with special needs who required extra care along with full-time therapy. And all of this was on top of balancing homeschool schedules while running two businesses. But she didn't know any of this yet.

"Wow!" I responded, gathering my thoughts as I determined the most polite way to decline such a coveted position. "While that sounds like a tremendous opportunity, and one that I would *really* enjoy, unfortunately, I'm not able to accept now."

I paused as her jaw dropped in shock and knew I had surprised her. Quickly regaining her composure, she nodded kindly, masking her disappointment. I went on to share more about my current situation—less to justify and defend than to inform—and found myself leaning in and building rapport, rather than creating distance.

We parted ways amicably, and I noticed that I felt lighter. Instead of adding more to my already full plate, I had set an intentional boundary to protect the needs of my time and my family. The practice of aligning my motivations with my actions allowed my values to fuel my choices: starting with getting really clear on my internal drivers that sustained my endurance.

Manage Your Motivators

Did you know that the average adult makes around thirty-five thousand decisions in a single day?[1] We possess genetic materials and chemical responses that help us discern environmental factors to distinguish what's good for us and what's not.

- *Go to bed early or watch the next episode?*
- *Head to the grocery store or go out to dinner?*
- *Go on vacation now or invest in retirement?*

Every choice we make is inherently motivated by specific factors: our needs, wants, goals, and even our fears—some consciously and many subconsciously. Which is why it's essential to understand the relationship between our emotions and motivations that influence what and how we choose.

I first learned about the science of motivation in my undergraduate Introduction to Psychology class. A decade later, I married a behavior analyst and soon became a parent, receiving a *true education* in motivation! Studying the core functions of behavior,[2] I discovered that most of our situational responses fall into these four categories:

1. **Attention:** Desiring to be noticed by someone
2. **Access:** Wanting a tangible object or experience
3. **Avoidance:** Trying to escape or get away from something or someone
4. **Automatic:** Doing something because it feels good

Now let's look at some everyday examples alongside the driving motivators:

- You prioritize spending more time with your child who has recently been acting out to get a reaction (*attention*).
- While you may really want to eat those cookies, you choose carrots instead to make healthier choices (*access*).
- You decide to clean your house instead of calling back the friend who hurt your feelings (*avoidance*).
- You choose to stay up late to keep reading the next chapter of the book you can't put down (*automatic*).

Every behavior has a purpose. And every choice has a consequence.

Every behavior has a purpose. And every choice has a consequence. By uncovering the motivation behind our behavior, we can understand what is driving our decisions.

Define Your Drivers

We all have certain internal and external factors—relationships, resources, and responsibilities—that influence our motivation and ability to make decisions and lead change. Some are positive *driving* forces that propel us forward, while others are negative *restraining* forces that pull us backward. Social psychologist Kurt Lewin modeled this as a force field where the goal is to maintain equilibrium.[3] Applying this concept, take a moment to map your own decisions:

What is positively motivating you now? Is this something coming from inside you or from around you?

- Inside you = Internal driving force
- Around you = External driving force

Now consider what's been holding you back. What negative self-talk or behaviors are you engaging in? What relationships and circumstances restrain your growth?

- Self = Internal restraining force
- Environment = External restraining force

When we notice our driving forces and restraining forces, we can make intentional changes that honor our priorities and values.

Activate Your Agency

When I declined the position to serve on the leadership board, I intentionally protected my time so I could be present with my family. My "no" wasn't hard because I had already reflected on my personal priorities and felt a sense of control over my choice. Psychologists call this sense of power your individual *agency*: the ability to act independently and make your own decisions.[4] Activating your agency takes intentionality, discernment, and self-regulation—which are all core skills you've already practiced as you increase your emotional endurance.

But what happens when we feel a loss of control or lack of influence? It all comes down to where we place our power.

Individuals who believe that luck, fate, or external circumstances have control over their lives tend to be more pessimistic and give up easily. This *external locus of control* feeds into a victim mentality and lack of personal agency when facing challenges or setbacks. In contrast, other individuals feel a sense of personal power and control over their actions, effort, and choices. They use this *internal locus of control* to work toward goals with purpose and optimism.[5]

So where does faith fit in? Since we were intentionally designed with free will to make decisions, we can trust that our ways will be guided and established.[6] We were not given a spirit of fear of the unknown but a spirit of strength, love, and peace.[7] Instead of being ruled by FOMO—the Fear of Missing Out that often delays decision-making—we can embrace JOMO, finding *joy* in the extra time we have to experience all that life has given us. If you are struggling now, may you find encouragement in knowing you have both the agency and ability to choose.

There's More to Your Story

Remember that pivotal phone call I told you about? Well, here's the next (and the best) part of that story:

After that call, my friend and I continued talking daily as I explored what my life could become in the season ahead. He encouraged me to pursue building my coaching practice and becoming my own boss instead of seeking the safety of a traditional career. To try. To risk. To start before I felt ready.

As we continued to pray together daily, he held me

accountable as I stayed focused and faithful. I had to be okay with *not* knowing what the future held as I shifted my perspective toward what was possible: to activate the resilience to rise so I could develop my emotional endurance.

The prayers I had the courage to pray in a season of such brokenness were fulfilled in a way I never thought possible.

From lying on my red couch to standing in a white wedding dress just six months later, I vowed to love and support the same man who had called to check in on me. I went from hopeless and exhausted to marrying someone I had known for a majority of my life and already had a profound respect for, all because I was willing to be led and follow.

The very best decisions in my life came when God moved before me (and I got out of His way). This required me to be keenly self-aware of my tendency to activate my own ideas instead of waiting on God's timing. He needed me to learn how to trust in faith in my lowest and hardest moments so He had room to move first: to stop seeking approval and attention and choose a renewed mind and transformed life.[8] And God had to physically move me halfway around the world to do it!

Less than a month into marriage, another unexpected phone call changed my life. When the foundation director at an international nonprofit invited us to serve abroad in the Middle East, we had to work together to define our shared drivers and values. As we prayed for wisdom and discernment, it became clear that God had been preparing our lives for such a time as this. Before the end of the year, we had moved to Amman,

Jordan, and started a new chapter of our story together. Expanding my territory took on a whole new meaning!

God didn't want me to play small or stay stuck any longer. And that's not your story either.

The world needs your gift. Start by stepping away from the brick wall so you can shift your perspective. Replace the fear of the unknown with the agency to make resonant choices. Get clear on what purpose is driving your decisions. From that empowered place, you can find the resilience to rise.

REFLECT + CONNECT

Considering the present season of your life, identify your core drivers and how they are currently operating to support your success.

- What are the biggest driving (*positive*) and restraining (*negative*) forces in your life now?
- Do you typically operate from an internal or external locus of control?
- If you could do one thing today that would boost your motivation, what would it be?

PRINCIPLE THREE

HOPE TO HEAL

Once we experience failure and rise up with resilience, we often feel a bit raw and maybe even a little uncertain of the pathway forward. We desire something greater, yet we often don't know how to access hope during trying times. **Harnessing hope to heal provides purpose and trajectory**, especially when the future still feels fuzzy. By applying Hope Theory and creating more margin in our lives, we realign with a bigger vision for what is possible. Let's look at what we can learn about hope from science and Scripture as we increase our emotional endurance.

SKILL 7

WAIT, WANDER, AND WONDER

"Coffee just doesn't sound good."

My husband looked at me with raised eyebrows and a smirk, shaking his head.

This phrase had come out of my mouth only two times before in the first decade of our marriage.

You see, I don't just *like* coffee. I full-on *love* coffee. Making and enjoying a perfect cup of coffee is part of my morning (and sometimes afternoon) routine, and it grounds my day. Combine coffee with a few quiet moments for prayer and spiritual study, and then I can pretty much take on anything!

So when my appetite for coffee is gone, it can mean only one thing.

Those two pink lines confirmed my hunch. Our family of four would prepare to welcome a fifth member, and I would go without coffee, yet again, for many weeks.

I'll never forget the day I found out I was pregnant with our daughter. It was March 16, 2020. The same day California received the first of many "shelter in place" orders as the COVID-19 pandemic began. Yet in the middle of the fear and uncertainty felt by so many, I wasn't afraid. In fact, the peace and hope I felt was utterly uncharacteristic given the circumstances we were heading into as a family and society.

At the start of 2020, I was running two small businesses—one being a brand-new coworking space with childcare that our family had opened only a year before—so there was a lot of uncertainty with what would happen next. Going headfirst into stay-at-home orders while being self-employed was entering unfamiliar territory without a guidebook. For some, the pandemic was the deciding factor in closing their businesses for good, changing careers, or going into early retirement.

But that was not our path.

Together, my husband and I made the intentional choice to continue operating, navigating uncertainty in business and pregnancy. Reflecting on this pivotal moment, there was one thing I knew with absolute certainty: God had brought this precious new life into ours at the perfect, appointed time. Already raising two young boys, we had been trying, praying, and waiting for another baby for years. During this season of ambiguity and anticipation, our Creator was using our story to grow something else in us. Something that would prepare us as parents and partners in this dynamic dance of life—especially when the tempo was about to change!

The months leading up to birth were hard as we expanded our business model to operate a full-day preschool program so we could serve more "essential workers": those designated by the government to maintain critical services during the pandemic. We went through periods of hustle and holdup as the external environment around us changed frequently with new requirements, updated health regulations, and best practices for early childhood education.

Our oldest son started kindergarten on Zoom and learned to read.

Our middle son was diagnosed with autism and began behavior therapy.

Our daughter "sheltered in place" in the womb as my hopes and dreams for our family, business, and community grew with her.

Our lives continued in a familiar cadence as we showed up for work each day to serve and support local families. We had a compelling reason to get our young children ready and out the door while our neighbors worked remotely or logged on to distance learning. This consistent purpose helped us find a rhythm and sense of stability in the most uncertain of times.

We finally welcomed our sweet Eden Rose into the world on Thanksgiving Day 2020—a true gift of gratitude as we expanded our family. Her birth felt like a culmination of so many things and finally gave me some precious time to simply be at home—an ironic fact as most of the world wanted to do anything *but* be stuck at home! While nurturing a newborn, I was able to reflect on the year we had lived and the burdens and blessings we had experienced. This new life gave us the hope we needed to heal so we could move forward in faith.

Wait on Hope

When we have hope in something or someone, we are able to envision a better and brighter future. Whatever we are facing in the present doesn't seem as heavy and hard. We can exhale, rest, and abide, so we can recover. We can begin healing from past hurts and handling present challenges because we have faith that what is to come will restore and refresh our lives.

What inspires your hope now?

Perhaps you've been suffering and long for healing and relief from your current condition.

Or maybe you have a desire for change, trusting in faith that your situation will improve soon.

And while prayers may be answered immediately, we are often left in seasons of waiting, wandering, and wondering when things will get easier or feel lighter while our burdens seem too heavy to bear. We read countless examples of miraculous and immediate healings in the Bible. Yet do we recognize that many of these people waited for relief for years—decades even—before their circumstances changed?

- A man who had been blind since birth received his sight after obediently following Jesus' instructions.[1]

- A woman who dealt with a continuous flow of blood for twelve years was healed by the single touch of a garment.[2]
- A man suffering with painful leprosy was cured and his health restored after humbling himself before his Savior.[3]

While the Bible says to find the joy in our trials as we grow our patience,[4] what happens when our patience wears thin while we long for the hope of healing?

These difficult seasons invite us to develop our emotional endurance where the work is in the waiting, wandering, and wondering. Here, we can remember the encouragement that "the Lord is not slow in keeping his promise, as some understand slowness. Instead he is patient with you, not wanting anyone to perish, but everyone to come to repentance" (2 Peter 3:9 NIV). To move forward with this hope, let's explore some key principles that open up new possibilities and pathways forward.

The work is in the waiting, wandering, and wondering.

Reclaim Your Power

It has often been said that "where there's a will, there's a way."

Maybe you have the will and inner resolve to fix the hard situation you're currently facing, but don't know where to start. If you could only figure out the first step forward, everything else might just fall into place.

What if we inverted this popular phrase and claimed that "where there's a *way*, there's a *will*"?

This is precisely what the late positive psychologist Charles Richard "Rick" Snyder studied to better understand people's ability to shape their futures. Fascinated with an individual's power to find and harness their internal motivation, Snyder wanted to understand what kept people going in the face of hardships and setbacks as well as what became possible once they found their purpose.

Snyder developed Hope Theory, which says hope is the perceived ability to produce strategies and forge new paths toward desired goals.[5] We can increase hope when we believe there's a way forward *and* can access new pathways toward opportunities we may have overlooked.

According to Snyder, there are two types of power that help us access more hope:

1. **Willpower:** Your inner motivation to work toward your goal and shape your future using Agency Thinking
2. **Waypower:** Your ability to see ways forward toward your desired goal using Pathways Thinking

If you know what you want but are lacking motivation, your *willpower* needs a boost.

If you have the inner desire but no clear pathways, your *waypower* needs a fresh perspective.

Individuals with emotional endurance know how to use their willpower and their waypower together as they work toward accomplishing their goals to access more hope. Yet we can't achieve either type of power in isolation. We need support and community to uncover new perspectives. We need motivation to go after our goals. And we need spiritual strength and eternal perspective as we wait, wander, and wonder.

Walk Out of the Wilderness

As I stood on Mount Nebo, overlooking the Dead Sea and the wilderness of Judea, a sense of peace washed over me. This was the promised land of the Old Testament—the very same geography that thousands of people risked their lives to enter, wandering for decades after fleeing Egyptian captivity. To the west flowed the Jordan River, the same water where Jesus was baptized centuries before.[6] I lifted my camera to immortalize the moment, but so much history could never be captured in a single snapshot.

Moses was 120 years old when he stood on this same mountain and announced to the Israelites that he would not lead them any farther.[7] After crossing the Red Sea, followed by decades of wilderness wandering, Moses had gone as far as he would go on this journey. He would not enter into the promised land.

Do you ever feel this way?

Maybe you have invested so much time, energy, and resources to get to where you are, only to be standing on top of the mountain—or even down in the valley—looking over at the vision of where you hoped to be already.

I imagine Moses felt a mixture of emotions that day.

- Joy for how far he had come.
- Peace in knowing that was as far as he would venture.
- Probably some disappointment when he realized he wouldn't go farther.
- And hope for the future for the people of Israel.

There is a type of healing that comes even when our hope is yet to be fulfilled.

God had prepared Joshua to lead the multitude across the Jordan River and into the land they had been promised, and Moses encouraged him with these memorable words: "Be strong and courageous. Do not be afraid or terrified because of them, for the LORD your God goes with you; he will never leave you nor forsake you" (Deuteronomy 31:6 NIV).

There is a type of healing that comes even when our hope is yet to be fulfilled.

Before Moses died, he recorded the entirety of the law, passing it on to the Israelites and to the generations to follow as they went ahead, entered the promised land, and claimed their inheritance.[8] As we wait, wander, and wonder, we can be encouraged by hope in an eternal inheritance. Not one that is bound by geography but one that transcends all history because of Jesus' ultimate sacrifice.[9]

REFLECT + CONNECT

Identify a goal or specific area of your life that you are ready to make progress in now.

- Determine your willpower and current motivation to achieve this goal.
- Now consider the various pathways and opportunities you can explore that expand your waypower. What feels possible here?
- How have your wilderness seasons increased your hope or ushered in healing?

SKILL 8

CREATE MARGIN TO RECOVER

In a moment of temporary insanity, we decided to travel to Europe when our children were seven, five, and almost two. We purchased a gently used jogging stroller and packed only two checked bags for our entire family (which I am still very proud of to this day!). As we unloaded at the airport and set up the stroller on the curb, I noticed that the tires seemed low. Dangerously low.

Once we added eighty pounds of children and gear to the stroller, it was apparent that all three tires were almost flat. The stroller was nearly impossible to push across the airport carpet. My willpower propelled me forward, but by the time we made it through security and to our gate, we were certain that irreparable damage had been done to at least one of the wheels.

Fast-forward twenty-four hours, where we found a bicycle shop on a street corner in Paris. With our tires full of air again, we rolled on with ease. But we *didn't* know it was possible to overinflate tires, which we soon discovered a few hours later. Standing below the twinkly lights of the Eiffel Tower, the first tire burst with a dramatic *pop!* The second tire blew shortly after on the walk back to the subway as we ate Nutella crepes under a Parisian full moon.

Navigating awkwardly with only one functional tire left, we made our way back to the hotel, silently regretting the albatross of a stroller we were stuck with for the next ten days. And while the third tire somehow made it through the entire trip—European cobblestones and all—our intentional stroller purchase looked pretty shabby by the time we returned home.

Why didn't you just check the tire pressure before we left? I chided myself multiple times as I pushed the jalopy of a stroller through quaint villages, train stations, and even more airports. This simple oversight significantly impacted our experience and reminded me of the dangers of overloading your days (or your stroller!) to the breaking point.

Consider the condition of the specific support structures present in your life. Have you checked your metaphorical tires recently? What do you need to do now to make sure you can keep rolling and moving forward? Let's explore the intersection between healing and hope, starting with how we can create and maintain margin in our lives.

Manage Your Margin

Dr. Richard Swenson noticed a profound and concerning pattern emerging in many of the patients who came to his private practice. They arrived at his office complaining of some type of pain that largely stemmed from a central issue: a lack of rest and peace because of their lifestyle. While the pain was the symptom of their overloaded lives, managing their margin was the necessary prescription for restoring their health. They needed more air in their tires.

"Margin grants freedom and permits rest," Dr. Swenson shared. "Margin is the space between our load and our limits. . . . It is the opposite of overload."[1] Dr. Swenson created a simple equation for determining how much margin you have in your life: **Power – Load = Margin.**

Your power includes all the things that allow you to accomplish your goals: energy, skills, time, training, strengths, faith, finances, and social support.

Your load includes anything that gets in the way: problems, obligations, work stressors, commitments, expectations, debt, deadlines, and interpersonal conflicts.[2]

When you subtract your load from your power, you are left with your available margin: your current capacity to help, serve, and contribute. Positive margin gives you time to be creative, collaborate, and rest. Here, we have space and ability

Positive margin gives you time to be creative, collaborate, and rest.

to serve and support others while taking care of ourselves with appreciation and kindness.

But what happens when our load outweighs our power, and we dip into negative margin? These are the times we get overwhelmed, and our capacity to deal with new stressors is stretched too far—our tires pop and our willpower evaporates. Feelings of frustration, anger, resentment, and guilt start to creep in, and we may even blame and shame others.

When we learn how to manage our margin, we are able to regain hope as we increase our emotional endurance. Just like a page has white space around the edges, our lives need margin—space that is not filled—so it can absorb some overflow or simply remain open so we can pause and rest. Here are some everyday examples of margin:

- Waking up rested and enjoying a cup of coffee or tea to welcome the day
- Finishing a project ahead of schedule with time to review it before the deadline
- Arriving early for a meeting or appointment
- Having a positive balance in your bank account
- Leaving the office at the end of the day on time and energized
- Making sure your stroller tires are fully inflated and ready to roll

And here's the opposite of margin:

- Feeling stressed and anxious
- Being rushed and reactive
- Always doing more without taking breaks
- Achieving tasks instead of investing in relationships
- Feeling constantly overwhelmed and burned-out
- Having flat or overfilled tires that could burst!

Take a moment to consider how your life would feel with more margin. Even if things are going fairly well now, imagine what may become possible if you had more space, time, energy, and breathing room. How would your life look and feel differently then? If you desire to lead a purpose-driven life that is grounded in your values, you must prioritize and protect your margin as you develop more emotional endurance.

Remember "Busy" Is Not a Badge of Honor

As seasoned multitaskers, we have become consumed with meeting and beating deadlines and raising the bottom line of our businesses while we raise our children, all while constantly creating and innovating. We react to what's in front of us and hustle to get more done. Our busyness turns to burnout. We rarely reflect on our lives because we are afraid of wasting time or falling

> *We sacrifice the art of being for the activity of doing.*

behind. And, in turn, we sacrifice the art of being for the activity of doing.

From traveling to over fifty countries, Dr. Swenson found that cultures who prioritized achievement and progress like our Western society had the least amount of margin.[3] This likely isn't shocking or surprising. Yet it should be concerning. If the way we are living and achieving isn't bringing lasting fulfillment, is this really how we should measure our success?

When I've asked my coaching clients to describe success, the most resonant responses come from a deep place of purpose. They share statements like these:

- "Success is being available for my children and family."
- "Success is knowing my work matters and has meaning."
- "Success is doing my best in school to develop skills for my future career."
- "Success is feeling alive and engaged in my job."
- "Success is serving in my community and helping those who have great need."

Yet these same thoughtful individuals often lead very full lives that have limited margin. They wear "busy" like a badge of honor. Author and podcast host Emily P. Freeman agrees that "busy is our default. Margin takes intention."[4] As I've coached, trained, and empowered thousands of individuals to lead with intention, I've noticed their hesitation to let go of being busy. If they stopped producing, serving, creating, and performing, what would they have left? What would define them then?

When we are operating with negative margin for a prolonged period of time, we can't live out our purpose because we simply have nothing left to give. At its core, margin is about being available **mentally**, **emotionally**, **physically**, and **spiritually**.

Choose Hope over Hustle

Our society moves at a breakneck pace, valuing efficiency and achievement over sufficiency and rest. But we weren't designed to live at the speed of light. As physical beings, we can hold only so much before we start getting tired, stressed, and stretched to our max. We sell out on sufficiency for the currency of efficiency. But at what cost? Imagine what would happen if we chose to prioritize sufficiency, margin, and healing instead of hustling.

We sell out on sufficiency for the currency of efficiency.

There are seasons for production and seasons for rest. The agrarian society of ancient Israel was instructed *not* to glean from the corners of their fields and to let the soil rest as a sabbath every seventh year so it was prepared and refreshed for the next harvest.[5] The intentionality of knowing what *not* to do creates necessary space in our lives, showing how there are appointed times and seasons for everything—including rest.[6]

While we are working hard to bear fruit, we are also told to be still and abide.[7] The spiritual practice of seeking solitude occurs throughout history and is modeled countless times by our Savior. While teaching the disciples and a multitude of followers, Jesus continually sought time away to quiet His life and seek the Father.[8] He stopped, prayed, reflected, and rested.

And we're invited to do the same. Whether it's a few deep breaths during a stressful part of our morning commute or setting aside more dedicated time for prayer and Bible study, learning how to quiet our lives so we can really listen to what we need is essential. By doing less—but doing it better—we create the capacity to handle life's pressures and stresses with emotional endurance, restoring hope with more air in our tires and margin in our lives.

REFLECT + CONNECT

Use the questions below to determine the amount of available margin in your life now:

- Consider your current personal power (energy, skills, time, training, strengths, faith, finances, and social support) and assign it a number between 1 and 10.
- How heavy does your load feel now? Assign it a number between 1 and 10.
- Now subtract your load from your power to determine your available amount of margin. How does this feel compared to what you desire?

SKILL 9

ENVISION YOUR FUTURE

Scanning the room, I smiled at the eager faces of the emerging leaders who had arrived for their program orientation. Within the auditorium at one of California's largest state agencies, many participants had just met each other for the first time as they embarked on this program together for the next six months.

"Good morning!" I cheerfully welcomed the group. "Let's start by getting to know each other better." As the program facilitator, I began introducing a popular team-building exercise called "Two Truths and a Lie," where individuals share two true things about themselves and one thing that's not true, and then others try to guess which one is the lie.

Now, as someone who was taught from a young age *not* to lie (plus, my poker face is terrible), I chose to put a fresh and more honest spin on the activity by rebranding it "Two Truths and a *Dream*." Instead of coming up with a lie, I asked participants to share two things they had done already and one thing they dreamed of doing someday. This could be a goal they'd set or something on their bucket list. Then their partner would guess which one was the dream as they got to know each other.

Can you guess mine?*

1. I have played the flute for over three decades.
2. I have been to as many countries as I am years old.
3. I have never broken a bone.

As participants started sharing, excited chatter filled the room. Shifting the narrative away from lying and deception toward aspiration and goal setting naturally elevated the energy of the group. Reframing the exercise for attendees to think of a dream—rather than one more thing they hadn't done yet—did something to inspire more possibility for the future. To hope. To heal. To move forward toward a goal or dream.

Redefine Success

"I am such a failure! This wasn't supposed to happen!"

I watched one of the strongest women I knew melt into a puddle of defeat as she recounted a situation that didn't turn out the way she expected after investing over a year of hard work. As an executive leader at a Fortune 500 company, she managed

* Reading through my list, you might have guessed that I'm still a few countries shy of my lifetime travel goal (#2 was my dream!). And did anyone really guess #3? Because breaking a bone is no one's dream!

a budget bigger than the GDP of some developing nations yet still could not escape a human reaction to disappointment.

After listening to her process her experience, I affirmed what I heard with some encouragement. "That sounds really hard and also *good* because you recognize you still have more to learn."

She looked shocked. Instead of accepting the invitation to her pity party, I held space for her emotions and acknowledged that she was still a beautiful work in progress.

Many of us struggle with this profound challenge: **dealing with the emotional gap between success and failure**, especially when that failure occurs in an area where we feel confident. Rather than tracking the small wins and progress we make toward a goal, we judge and label our setbacks when we haven't accomplished what we intended.

Consider the vision you have for your life. What have you worked hard to achieve and haven't reached *yet*? What do you hope to accomplish one day but aren't there *yet*?

When we view achieving success on a spectrum, we can clearly see the difference between interpreting defeat or rejection as "failure" instead of not succeeding *yet*. Remember, a lack of success is not equivalent to failure. Rather, in the right headspace, a "not yet" success becomes an invitation to learn, grow, and develop. Then we can redefine a vision for success based on progress rather than reaching the end product.

> *A lack of success is not equivalent to failure. Rather, it becomes an invitation to learn, grow, and develop.*

The areas in your life that you may have automatically assigned as "failures" are actually the raw potential for your future success. **Instead of dwelling on what hasn't happened yet, recognize what is working for you now, along with the potential for future growth.** As we get clear on what's possible in the present, we discover the large gap of "not yet" that exists between the bookends of failure and success. And suddenly "not yet" becomes fuel for hope.

Become a Solution Seeker

Instead of focusing on what isn't working, try reframing the situation to see what's possible now. Research has found that using reflective visioning exercises to focus on what you want success to look like improves goal clarity, motivation, and resilience.[1] Shifting your focus from being a *problem solver* to becoming a *solution seeker* allows you to explore new opportunities. Here's how I like to think of it:

Problem Solving = Weakness Fixing

Solution Seeking = Strength Building

Failure continues only when we refuse to try, learn, pray, and practice.

We're stuck only when we stop looking for solutions. When we accept feeling lost or behind as an invitation to become a student of what life is teaching us *now*, we build our capacity for what's *next*.

We listen.
We pause.
We approach the unexpected situation as a chance to learn.
We continue refining our skills so we have a shot at the next big opportunity.
We become solution seekers who look toward the future with more vision and purpose.

Capture Your Glimmers

Do the thing that makes you come alive.

The words were drawn in fancy script on a shop window at a neighborhood boutique selling kitchen gadgets and handmade gifts. I smiled at the thought, then paused to consider the questions that emerged: *What makes me come alive? How does this inspire my hope?*

Since we own and operate a childcare center on top of our parenting responsibilities, most of my days are spent attending to the needs of other people. When I am swamped with a full calendar of meetings, deadlines, and carpool routes, I have to protect my margin and find moments that fuel me: belly laughs from our young daughter, Eden, or bear hugs from our middle son, Luke, fill me up fully, renewing my energy and sparking my joy. These are welcome reminders that my days are well spent, and I have a beautiful life amid my ongoing tasks and obligations. These are my *glimmers* of hope.

According to licensed clinical social worker Deb Dana, the opposite of triggers are called "glimmers": moments of connection that cue our nervous system to feel safe and calm.[2] Our glimmers don't need to be great, big, expansive experiences of joy, safety, or connection. Rather, they are micro moments that begin to shape our lives in very gentle ways. Our oldest son, Caleb, shared the best definition of glimmers I've heard, calling them "a sparkle of joy." Here are some of the glimmers I've noticed recently:

- *A beautiful sunrise on a morning walk*
- *The delicate latte art on the top of a cup of coffee*
- *Messy toddler crafts made "just for Mama"*

Like capturing fireflies in a jar on a sticky summer night, noticing and appreciating these glimmers helps us hold sacred space for what lights us up. Glimmers have so many positive benefits on our physical, emotional, and spiritual lives, helping us reconnect our vision with a sense of peace and security. These experiences allow our bodies, minds, and souls to regulate as we feel more relaxed and at ease, safe and protected. And as we intentionally look for glimmers and give them our attention, we tend to notice them more and more. Savoring these small moments of joy builds our inner capacity to face whatever is ahead with more hope as we live out our vision.

Choose a Hope-Filled Future

Remember that phone call that changed my life and led to me marrying my best friend? While it may seem like the plot of a popular rom-com, I actually experienced a lot of challenging years of healing between that call over a decade ago and the arrival of our third baby in the middle of a global pandemic. There were many days when I had to convince myself to get out of bed because I felt so physically and emotionally weak. Days when it was easier to avoid doing hard things because the risk of losing something else felt *too* great. Days and days and days when I would have given anything just to feel better.

Maybe you can relate.

If you're suffering now and have been for a while, I invite you to rest in this promise: There is hope in healing, even and especially in the middle of the suffering. Find space to rest in hope as you travel though the "not yet" seasons of life. Remember, healing often is not immediate, yet it is always right on time—in God's time.[3]

There is hope in healing, even and especially in the middle of the suffering.

When we feel worn out, broken down, and just plain tired, God sees us as so much more and restores our hope: "May the God of hope fill you with all joy and peace as you trust in him, so that you may overflow with hope by the power of the Holy Spirit" (Romans 15:13 NIV). The promise of restoration and this eternal hope in something greater serve as the pillars of fire guiding us through the darkness of our wilderness seasons. We find hope in an even greater reward that gives our life vision and purpose.[4]

REFLECT + CONNECT

As you reflect on the vision you have for your life, consider the following:

- What is a dream you desire to accomplish?
- What glimmers are you noticing now?
- What have your hard times taught you about hope and healing?

PRINCIPLE FOUR

COURAGE TO CHANGE

It takes courage and consistency to continue on the path of transformation, especially when we may not see immediate results. A deeper neurological understanding shows how **we are designed to be brave and have the capacity to grow, develop, and overcome**. Yet change is still hard, especially as we recognize our blind spots and grow in self-awareness. Let's learn how the science of mindset and Scripture help us exercise the courage to change.

SKILL 10

SAY GOODBYE TO SOMEDAY

Once upon a time in a land far, far away, there were two kingdoms that were constantly fighting. In the Land of Could, the citizens spent their time daydreaming about all the things they *could* do in a world filled with so many possibilities. Their neighbors in the Land of Should often criticized the people of Could for being unrealistic and unproductive.

Instead of focusing on the future, the citizens of Should were keenly aware of everything they needed to do in the present. Their daily obligations left them little time to consider what else they truly wanted in their lives. They ended each day exhausted and anxious about all the things they still *should* complete.

Right off the coast was a beautiful island with pristine beaches and endless hours of sunlight. Driven by restlessness and burnout, citizens from both kingdoms would vacation there to escape the pressures of their daily lives. On the island they were able to ignore their negative thoughts as they thrived off the collective energy of all their dreams and ambitions. This magical place was fondly called Someday Isle.

Trading in their endless to-do lists for fruity drinks with colorful umbrellas, vacationers talked about all the things that would happen *someday* when their lives were different. Someday Isle was neutral ground for both kingdoms. But even with the constant buzz of ideas, future plans, and big dreams, an unspoken understanding existed among the travelers: They knew that after the vacation was over, they needed to leave the island.

Leave the Island

When life feels heavy and hard, it's tempting to travel to Someday Isle, telling ourselves we can get through whatever is in our way now because *Someday, I'll . . .*

- *Have a better job*
- *Find the perfect partner*
- *Buy a bigger house*
- *Exercise more*
- *Be enough*

How often do we put conditions on our present happiness by existing in the future of unfulfilled expectations? Or maybe we choose *not* to start something because we're uncertain or afraid of what might happen. So many people stay stuck in their coulds, shoulds, and somedays.

So many people stay stuck in their coulds, shoulds, and somedays.

Instead of embracing the courage to change, it's much easier to stay on the sunny shore of Someday Isle where we can daydream about how our lives *could* or *should* be different without putting in the effort now.

Consider how often you are . . .

- **dwelling** on what you can't change
- **ruminating** over something you are worried about
- **forecasting** all the negative possibilities of what could happen

In order to move forward, we must be willing to leave the island and reengage with reality, choosing an attitude of humility and bravery. Together, let's make the choice to get out of our beach chair, brush the sand from our toes, and return to reality.

Embrace the Courage to Change

Think back to a time when you felt courageous.

- *Where were you?*
- *What was happening?*
- *Who were you with?*
- *How did you feel?*

Now notice anything that *wasn't* present that allowed you to access more courage. Maybe certain limiting beliefs were silent or specific unsupportive individuals weren't around to discourage you. I would venture a guess that the *shoulds* and *coulds* that kept you stuck on Someday Isle were silent in this brave space.

Courage is the willingness to act in the face of fear, uncertainty, and doubt.

When we break down this definition, we see that courage is more than our circumstances and involves two core aspects:

1. Being willing to *make change happen* through positive action
2. Having the ability to *manage negative emotions* to sustain desired change

Moments of courage define our sense of self and shape our path forward. Clinical ethicist and researcher Michele DeMarco shares that "courage is found in the quiet moment between stimulus and response." She goes on to say that we find courage "only when we keep ourselves in a grounded, intentional place of confidence and choice by metabolizing fear."[1] When navigating my own life changes, I have discovered a new side of courage that shows up more like a steady friend who sits quietly beside you, cheering you on.

The Bible is filled with examples of ordinary people exercising courage to do extraordinary things:

- Moses approached a bush that was on fire yet would not burn up, unsure of what would unfold.[2]
- David battled the giant Goliath with just a slingshot and his faith in a God he trusted yet could not see.[3]

- Daniel was thrown in a den of hungry lions after refusing to stop praying to the God he served.[4]
- Esther became queen and approached the king without permission—something that could have cost her life—in order to save a nation.[5]

All of these biblical examples showcase courage as a core character trait of these faithful individuals. But did you know that you were intentionally designed to live and lead with courage? Brain science shows us how.

Know You're Wired for Courage

Our brain was intentionally designed for bravery to help us survive in the middle of chaos and confusion. Dr. Andrew Huberman, an associate professor of neurobiology and ophthalmology at Stanford University School of Medicine, discovered specific brain circuits that influence our choice either to fight or flee in the face of danger.[6]

This means that as a cognitive ability, courage can be strengthened over time because of the brain's neuroplasticity—our amazing ability to adapt to internal and external stimuli so we can change and reorganize our brain by forming new neurological connections.

And many areas of our brain work together to make courage possible:

The **prefrontal cortex** (PFC) is our brain's executive center that is responsible for emotional regulation,

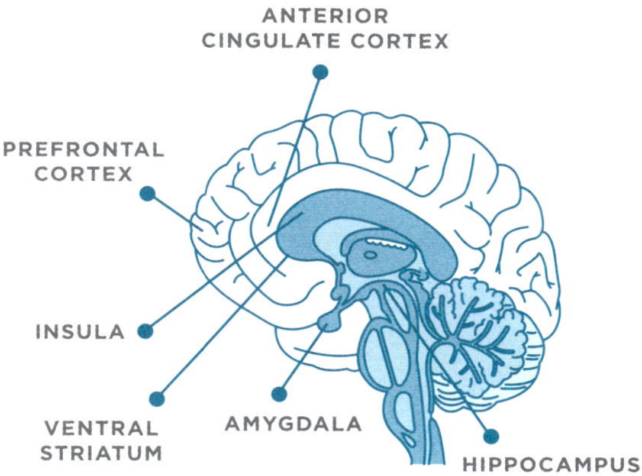

impulse control, and decision-making. It helps us weigh potential risks and rewards so we can make better decisions in situations that require courage to act.

The **amygdala** is known as the brain's "fear center" and plays a vital role in processing emotions, particularly fear and anxiety that drive the automatic fight-or-flight response.

The **hippocampus** is our "memory center" that integrates past knowledge we have learned from experiences to help us develop more courage.

The **insula** is our "intuition center," helping us process our emotions as we evaluate potential threats.

The **anterior cingulate cortex** works to integrate information from many regions of our brain as we assess risks, regulate emotions, and suppress bodily fear responses.

The **ventral striatum** is our brain's "reward system," where the release of dopamine reinforces certain experiences and encourages us to continue to exercise bravery in the future.[7]

Courage increases when these areas of the brain work together, powered by neurotransmitters like adrenaline, dopamine, serotonin, and oxytocin.[8] With this scientific understanding of how we're intentionally wired for bravery, let's see what happens when we exercise courage and allow our emotions to soften so we become more open to change.

Soften Your Feelings

I watched our kids playing Jenga with their cousins around the dining room table. Just shy of three years old, Eden insisted on joining the "big kids," even though her stubby fingers weren't quite as steady as the others'.

"Be careful," warned the oldest cousin, trying to prevent the wooden tower from falling. Inevitably, as Eden tried to get one of the middle blocks out, the tower came crashing down! She looked devastated, and her older brother quickly noticed.

"It happens," Caleb said with understanding as he picked up the scattered Jenga blocks from the floor. "No hard feelings," he added with a shrug and a smile.

Eden's demeanor instantly shifted from sadness to curiosity. "But what about soft feelings?" she asked with wide eyes.

Soft feelings? Her innocent question made me pause to consider what the difference might be.

Hard feelings are rigid and rooted in anger and bitterness. They often don't change easily and grow stronger with time because of a need to defend or prove something.

Soft feelings require vulnerability, authenticity, and a willingness to flex. They lead to moments of deep connection and collaboration as we exercise courage with empathy.

When we choose to show up with our soft feelings, we do not need to be right or have all the answers. Activating courage requires the ability to be vulnerable enough to recognize when we don't know it all or to discover areas where we need to change. Author and researcher Brené Brown affirms that "courage starts with showing up and letting ourselves be seen."[9] Here, with our shaky towers, we allow our weakest parts to be witnessed. In this place of vulnerability, we are more open to listen, be curious, and exercise the courage to change our own viewpoints because of what we learn with and from others.

Activate Your Courage

When life feels much like a game of Jenga, refusing to harden our feelings is crucial to staying present and connected in relationships. It's the only way our tower will grow taller, even if it doesn't appear as strong. When we're trying our best to make our next move and build with what we have, our soft feelings help us move slower, listen more, and intentionally respond. The Bible tells us to be quick to listen, to be slow to speak, and to humble ourselves so we can put God's Word into action.[10] It's not enough to know what to do; we have to get out there and do it with the right attitude and focus.

When approaching uncertainty and seasons of change, keeping our feelings soft and remaining teachable allows us to lean into the vulnerability to learn, grow, and overcome. Otherwise, we stay stuck on Someday Isle, digging our toes in the sand with hard feelings and heavy hearts. Becoming brave and choosing to say goodbye to your *somedays* moves you into intentional action toward the vision you have set as you continue on with emotional endurance.

REFLECT + CONNECT

Take a moment to identify an area in your life where you desire more change now.

- Note any *shoulds*, *coulds*, or *somedays* that you've been using as excuses to avoid getting started.
- What would it look like to be brave here? Notice what becomes possible when you choose courage over fear.
- Now consider if you have any hard feelings that need to soften. What do you need to release or retire to move forward?

SKILL 11

MANAGE YOUR MINDSET

Contemporary jazz played through my Bluetooth speaker as I started making Sunday brunch. I took a sip of coffee and smiled as my husband, Joel, came downstairs and reached for his mug with a quick good morning kiss. We had been married only two weeks, and those moments were still so fresh and sweet.

"Anything I can help with?" he asked with a sleepy smile.

I was used to cooking solo and hadn't gotten accustomed to delegating in the kitchen. After pausing to scan the counter, I handed him a bunch of overripe bananas. "It would be great to freeze these for smoothies," I said, and then I resumed chopping veggies for our omelets.

Less than a minute later, I turned back to the sink to rinse the cutting board and stopped in my tracks. "What are you doing?!"

I must have looked at Joel with crazy eyes because he just stared back, puzzled. "Freezing the bananas?" His words came out more like a question than a statement.

"You're supposed to peel them, then cut them into thirds. That's the only way they'll freeze correctly."

I realized my error as the words came out: I had created an arbitrary method for the "right" way to do this task that wasn't universally understood.

And thankfully, Joel simply smiled back, holding my gaze as he slowly shook his head without saying a word. The bananas remained whole in the Ziploc bag (but at least they were peeled). Perfect for future smoothies.

That Sunday, we developed one of our first "marriage codes." Now when we find ourselves stuck in a mindset where we assume there's one right way to do something (and it's typically mine), one of us will say, "You're driving me bananas" or simply the shorthand, "bananas." This is generally followed by a laugh that immediately defuses the anger and allows us to reconnect.

Maybe you've had your own moments where you're going bananas. Then it's time to manage your mindset!

Be Mindful of Mindset

Your *mindset* is the mental framework you adopt that selectively organizes and encodes information, shaping how you engage with and understand the world around you. Carol Dweck, preeminent mindset researcher and professor of psychology at Stanford University, contends that "mindsets are an important part of your personality, but you *can* change them."[1] Decades of research by Dweck and her team reveal how people of all ages and in various stages of life embody two distinctly different ways of viewing the world, either with a *fixed mindset* or a *growth mindset*.

Those who choose a *fixed mindset* focus on outcomes. They assume that if you possess natural talent, you will succeed. And if you fail or don't get what you want, it's because you weren't smart or good enough to begin with. When operating with a fixed mindset, success isn't about learning—it's about proving yourself. The accomplishments of others feel threatening, and feedback isn't welcome. You must be the best or else you're never enough. Some may choose to do nothing at all so they don't risk failure or defeat.

QUALITIES OF A FIXED MINDSET	QUALITIES OF A GROWTH MINDSET
You believe intelligence is innate	You believe you can always learn more
You avoid challenges for fear of failure	You embrace challenges as opportunities
You give up easily	You persist in the face of setbacks
You ignore constructive criticism	You seek out feedback to learn and grow
You avoid uncomfortable situations	You try novel things
You have a drive to continually achieve to prove worth	You understand your worth isn't based on your accomplishments
You feel threatened by the success of others	You champion the success of others

On the neurological flip side, choosing a *growth mindset* allows you to value your investment of time, energy, and skill regardless of what happens. Where you begin is just a starting point—not the end result. With a growth mindset, you embrace the "not yet" as an invitation for future growth. The processes of learning and developing are what matter most. Individuals who choose a growth mindset are marked by their perseverance and resilience along with the flexibility to change.[2]

Adopt a Growth Mindset

How you think influences who you become.

- *How do you view yourself?*
- *Has your self-perception changed over time?*
- *Are you proud of who you are now?*

The answers to these questions reveal the underlying mindset you've chosen to embody, especially during times of transition, uncertainty, and setback. Research on mindset science has revealed one consistent finding: You have the ability to choose how you view yourself and others. Which is why it is crucial to understand what influences our mindset as we activate the courage to change.

You have the ability to choose how you view yourself and others.

Psychologist and researcher Kari Leibowitz spent a year studying the mindsets of Norwegians residing above the Arctic Circle. These Norwegians were living in total darkness during a two-month period when the sun never rises. Leibowitz's research found that a positive wintertime mindset was associated with *every* metric of well-being, including life satisfaction, positive emotions, psychological flourishing, and personal growth, among others.[3]

Simply put, **choosing a positive mindset had a direct correlation with happiness and well-being**, even when faced with the harshest circumstances. From this research, a new angle of mindset science emerged, demonstrating that choosing to change what you think in a certain area (single-belief intervention) can shift your mindset to bring about improvements in wellness, happiness, and success—even for years to come.[4]

These same truths have been around for centuries. In the Bible, the apostle Paul wrote a letter to the church in Philippi, Greece, encouraging them with these words: "Whatever things are true, whatever things are noble, whatever things are just, whatever things are pure, whatever things are lovely, whatever things are of good report, if there is any virtue and if there is anything praiseworthy—meditate on these things" (Philippians 4:8 NKJV).

And can you guess where Paul was when he wrote these powerful and positive words? In a Roman prison! He wasn't free to preach the gospel in person, but that didn't stop Paul from writing to the people he had met along his missionary journey to encourage and remind them that they could choose what they focused on, even if they couldn't change their circumstances.

You are not stuck in your situation, even if it feels that way at times. You are creative and resourceful, able to manage your mindset based on what you choose to focus on. Don't surrender to your circumstances. Choose your perspective with purpose and intention. While things may not immediately change, how you view them shifts when you have the courage to change your mental attitude.

You are not stuck in your situation.

View Setbacks as Setups

One day you're on a path forward, making progress and feeling good about the trajectory of your life. Then the next day, something unexpected happens and you get stuck or stalled out, lacking energy, motivation, and hope. But what if these setbacks are simply opportunities that set you up for what's next? They're all part of the larger purpose for who you need to become in order for God to use you for His greater glory!

A few years ago, I shifted my mindset to *viewing setbacks as setups*, and it has changed my perspective on progress, allowing me to identify the blessings that came from experiencing the burdens. So when unexpected or unwanted circumstances occur, they're not a stopping point—just another starting line. Here are some of mine:

- The main sewer line burst days after we moved our business into a new building, amounting to costly emergency repairs. The next month we learned that we had been selected for a grant to update the historic house, covering our plumbing expenses and other needed repairs.

- The truck we couldn't sell for months allowed us to bless a family member when they needed a reliable vehicle.
- The baby we prayed for didn't come for almost four years, allowing us focused time to intentionally parent our young child with special needs.

We may not know why something happens the way it does or why something hasn't happened yet, but God always knows.

He even put His master plan for salvation in motion using a teenage girl and a miracle birth! Even after living a perfect life, Jesus was betrayed for thirty pieces of silver and then crucified, leaving His faithful followers wondering why. For three days, they mourned the loss of their beloved teacher and friend until Jesus was resurrected, fulfilling the messianic prophecy and providing hope in a future glory.[5] Can you imagine if Jesus, while in His human form on earth, had simply decided that the plan for salvation wasn't worth the suffering? Even our Savior was left with a choice. And He chose *you*.

Just like Jesus, you were designed with personal agency: the power to intentionally influence your life and manage and respond to whatever you face. While there is much you cannot change because you will never have full control, you can always trust that *God does*. He will never leave you nor forsake you.[6] Once you recognize what is simply beyond your reach based on your circumstances, you can take ownership of the rest with courage and conviction.

Having a fixed mindset gets in the way of our faith. Exercising the courage to continually show up in the face of challenges helps us maintain a growth mindset as we believe in a God bigger than the problems we are facing now.

REFLECT + CONNECT

Take a moment to consider your current mindset and how it's shaping your choices.

- When facing problems, do you typically default to a fixed mindset or a growth mindset? How would the people closest to you describe you?
- Identify one area where you may have a fixed mindset and reframe it to access more courage. What is possible here?
- What is one setback you've experienced that set you up for something amazing that you never could have planned?

SKILL 12

EXPAND YOUR COMFORT ZONE

The highway ahead was dark, with no villages in sight on the long stretch of road back to Ephesus. Having moved to the Middle East just a few months before, Joel and I were exploring the biblical cities of Turkey as we celebrated our first wedding anniversary. To pass the time, I suggested something unconventional: "Since we have known each other for over half our lives, I think it would be fun to share what we've learned about each other in our first year of marriage."

Joel looked at me with knowing interest and an understanding that came from being lifelong friends before getting married. We spent the better part of the next hour taking turns sharing insights and reflections about each other and what changes we'd witnessed in our lives. Some remarks were funny, while others were more serious and thoughtful.

Then Joel said something I'll never forget.

"You like to be comfortable," he simply stated. Responding in obvious agreement, I nodded as he continued, "And I thrive when I'm *un*comfortable."

His words landed in a new way as I realized how we require exact opposite environments to find homeostasis. Growing up, I watched Joel compete in high-endurance sports that pushed and expanded his limits. While I love a grand adventure (especially when it involves travel and coffee), I would much rather host a dinner party with close friends or read a good book under a cozy blanket.

"But what I *also* realized," Joel said, continuing his thought, "is that by seeking physical comfort, you're able to take on much harder issues emotionally to help others."

Reflecting on this insight, I realized just how right he was. I purposefully design my life to maximize my physical comfort: from intentionally curating our home environment to wearing clothes that fit well and make me feel good. I also realized that, in doing so, I am able to handle extreme emotional discomfort because I have more capacity to support others when my physical needs are met.

But it hasn't always been this way.

At a young age, I learned certain coping strategies the hard way as my parents' fighting increased and my need for physical security rose to counterbalance the emotional insecurity I felt. Even then, the roots for developing my emotional endurance were growing deeper. Yet seeking comfort was never a lasting solution. We have been called to so much more.[1]

We don't build our emotional endurance in seasons of comfort. As we lean into our discomfort, we can access more courage and break down the lies and limiting beliefs in order to build back up again.

Check Your Blind Spot

One of the core skills I learned in driver's ed was how to change lanes, making sure to check my blind spot before merging. A decade later in graduate school, when I was studying identity formation, I started to unpack the related concept of personal blind spots: what others see in us, but we don't notice. As we gain awareness and choose to change, there is a complex interplay between our current level of *competence* (how well we do something) and our present awareness or *consciousness* (how much we currently know). This developmental process is outlined in the related conscious competence learning model.[2]

Self-discovery is a developmental process. At stage 1, you simply don't know what you don't know—like when my supervisor at the University of Illinois shared the hard truth that I needed to scale back my enthusiasm. Living out the popular axiom "Ignorance is bliss," you continue doing only what you know how to do, unaware of certain blind spots that may be inhibiting your success while you are **Unconsciously Incompetent**.

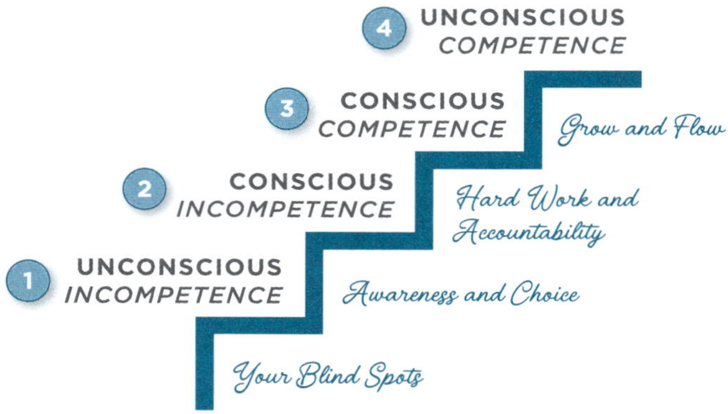

Stage 1. Unconscious Incompetence: You don't know what you don't know.

Stage 2. Conscious Incompetence: You become aware of a deficit you didn't recognize before.

Stage 3. Conscious Competence: You work hard to learn more and are continually seeking improvement.

Stage 4. Unconscious Competence: You have developed skills you now perform naturally without extra effort.

Then someone or something makes you aware of an area or skill that you are deficient in and you become **Consciously Incompetent**, entering stage 2. Often a well-intentioned mentor, friend, or family member may share feedback or constructive criticism with you, helping you gain awareness of an area to improve. This is where I found myself once I learned how others were perceiving my overeager behavior. Here, I was given the choice to accept this feedback and exercise the courage to change or stay stuck at this stage.

As you consciously choose to work on developing your skills, you enter stage 3 and become more **Consciously Competent**. This is the place where you double down on hard work and consistent effort to make the necessary changes. You may seek out a coach, mentor, therapist, close friend, or family member to provide support and make sure you don't regress. Consistency and accountability are key for growth at stage 3.

Over time, when you have practiced to the point where this behavior becomes a typical part of your routine, you become **Unconsciously Competent**. Once you reach stage 4, you're in a state of flow as things come more naturally—like riding a bicycle, signing your name, or taking a breath. All of the energy and effort you invested in the prior stages is integrated as you exercise this skill with ease and mastery.

Until you don't!

We all have moments when we unintentionally slip up and the learning process continues as we develop our emotional endurance. One passage in Scripture captures this inner battle well: "For what I am doing, I do not understand. For what I will to do, that I do not practice; but what I hate, that I do" (Romans 7:15 NKJV). Even when we know what to do, we still make mistakes because we're human and imperfect works in progress.

Growth often isn't linear. Our natural learning has a built-in feedback loop along with typical regression—especially when we are given feedback we don't expect or uncover blind spots we didn't realize we had. Change happens only when we respond once we recognize something new that we need to work on and commit to doing it. This process takes an immense amount of patience, honesty, humility, and courage because we are *always and continually learning*. Extend yourself some grace and recommit to making progress toward your goals with a growth mindset—and be willing to try out a different way.

Try It Backward

We've learned how behavior change occurs when we first name our emotions so we can manage how they shape our thoughts and actions. But did you know that change also happens when we simply choose to do something different even when we feel the same? In my most stuck times, I've had to first change *what* I'm doing before my brain understood *why* I was doing it. Obedience often precedes understanding.

Parents model this process when teaching their toddlers not to touch a hot surface or the importance of looking both ways before crossing the street. Young children don't fully understand the *why* behind their parents' instruction. They simply love and trust them, so they listen and (hopefully!) follow in obedience. As their cognitive function and emotional maturity develop, children begin to connect the dots and understand the *why* behind what they're taught. The boundaries are no longer seen as burdens—they're beacons shining a light toward the right way to go.

We see this same pattern in the Bible when God gave ancient Israel the Ten Commandments. God knew they, just like young children, needed order and structure to feel safe. After leaving

Egypt, the Israelites crossed the Red Sea into a type of freedom they had never experienced. Some felt so lost in the wilderness without the familiar comforts of captivity that they begged to go back to the safety of slavery.[3] But God had a different plan.

Meeting them in a place of deep loss and uncertainty, God allowed the Israelites to feel a myriad of emotions and even experience rebellion. While they still complained about the food and lack of comfort, their basic needs were always met as they were led forward into a future of prosperity.[4] Shining as a pillar of fire by night to light their path and a pillar of cloud by day to provide shade and protection, God showed them the way forward toward the promised land.[5]

When we're wandering without clear purpose in our own wilderness seasons, having some guidelines to light our path is crucial as we shift our behavior and change our mindsets. When we continue to practice new skills daily, they become more natural and automatic. But it still takes work and consistent effort to sustain the change we desire.

At this point most people get impatient. They think progress isn't being made fast enough and give up hope or lose interest. But dealing with the discomfort of slow change is the most crucial part of the process: **You keep going. You don't quit. You take the time to support the change you desire to see.**

Then once the behavior change finally occurs, you still don't stop. You continue practicing, modeling, and reinforcing the new behavior so regression doesn't occur. You're all in for the long haul, trusting that the God who brought the Israelites to the promised land will bring you through your own season of wandering.

We think we must know the *why* before we do the *what*. Yet that's just our human desire for comfort and control talking. Instead, adopting a humble attitude that is willing to consistently show up in the face of our challenges, uncertainty, and discomfort is what drives true and lasting change—motivating us to move beyond our comfort zone and wander in the wilderness as we keep learning with a growth mindset.

REFLECT + CONNECT

Consider your current comfort zone and your natural response to challenge that requires change:

- Think back to a time when you felt physically or emotionally uncomfortable. What did that experience teach you?
- Notice what specific blind spots you're becoming aware of in your life now. What are you choosing to do to change?
- When was a time that you had to first act in obedience before the change you desired occurred? Name what you learned.

PRINCIPLE FIVE

ENERGY TO ENGAGE

Just as we manage our time, **we can learn how to manage our energy in order to build emotional endurance**. In this section, we'll explore what drains our reserves and restores our margin by applying biblical wisdom to the science of energy management. We'll learn how to use stress as a positive motivator to expand our capacity to handle what's hard. Together, let's commit to staying present and engaged as we create healthy rhythms for our lives.

SKILL 13

ENHANCE YOUR ENERGY

I carefully set the large glass jar on the conference room table next to a pile of rocks and a bag of sand while the room of college students watched with skeptical interest. I was halfway through graduate school and supervising a team of student leaders in residential life, hoping to teach them a valuable lesson they wouldn't forget.

"Our lives can feel so busy," I began as I placed large rocks inside the jar. "From managing multiple academic classes, to your jobs as resident assistants—you have to be mindful and strategic in how you allocate your time. Then there are maintenance activities like laundry, showering, eating, and homework." I opened the bag of sand and poured it in the jar. The tiny grains filled in the gaps between the rocks, forming a small mountain on top.

Holding up the empty bag of sand, I picked up another big

rock and attempted to put it into the already full jar. "Then we get sick because we haven't slept enough," I added. While there was no visible room for the large rock, I set it on top of the mountain of sand anyway. "But getting sick wasn't part of the plan, and now life has to slow down to make space so we can rest and heal."

The students watched the large rock slowly sink beneath the pile of sand, pushing through until it completely disappeared.

"And as we recover, we continue on, packing our lives so full that we have no space for anything else," I said, gesturing first to the jar that was now filled to the brim and then to the pile of rocks still left on the nearby table. "But are we prioritizing the right things? How are we intentionally filling our lives?"

Now I had their attention. Picking up one of the large rocks from the table, I asked, "What are your big rocks? Those are the things you have to put in first before your life gets too full."

Their responses revealed their biggest priorities at this stage:

- *I'm a student athlete and need to train to stay in shape.*
- *I call my family to check in while I'm walking to class.*
- *I make sure my homework is done before I go out.*
- *I go to church every week.*

"When we make space for our big rocks first, we have more room for the rest," I added.

Then I picked up my coffee mug and slowly tipped it over the top of the jar. The dark liquid seeped through the sand, settling into spaces that weren't visible before. "But even when your lives feel full, there's always time for a cup of coffee, a phone call, a high five, or a deep breath. We should never be too busy for the people we care about or to care for ourselves." After pausing for effect while raising my empty mug, I added, "And when your jar feels too full, it's time to take a coffee break."

Now two decades later, I still have this phrase displayed on my desk in a bright blue coffee-mug-shaped picture frame that reminds me of this important truth: We have to prioritize our big rocks along with regular rest so our jars don't get too full.

Learn to Manage Your Energy

"Let me check my calendar and get back to you."

How many times have you responded to someone's invitation or request in a similar way? For some, keeping a full calendar brings control and order to their busy lives that are so full of activities and obligations. But what if I told you the secret to getting things done efficiently isn't time management?

Your performance, health, and happiness are grounded in how well you manage your *energy*—not your calendar!

Energy is our most important physical resource and the distinguishing factor for high performance. No matter how strategic you are, without knowing how to use your energy effectively, you still will feel drained, disconnected, and discouraged. When we choose how we invest our time and talent based on the energy outcome it produces, things dramatically change. Your time is finite. Your energy is renewable.

Your time is finite. Your energy is renewable.

When someone invites you to an event or asks you to help out with a task at work, normally you only think about how much time it will take. But saying yes also means you'll incur other costs that you may not have considered. For example:

- The *physical* cost and energy you'll expend on this activity
- The *emotional* cost of saying yes by adding another obligation to your plate
- The *mental* cost of making sure you understand all the details
- The *spiritual* cost of doing something mundane that may not contribute to your overall values or goals

Who knew there was so much energy at stake for one yes?

Performance psychologists Jim Loehr and Tony Schwartz devised a new paradigm for understanding how our decisions are impacted by four domains of energy: physical energy, emotional energy, mental energy, and spiritual energy.[1]

FOUR DOMAINS OF ENERGY

Physical energy is the amount of energy we're able to hold or achieve, given the sustainability of our load.

Emotional energy is the quality of our relationships, based on the level of security we perceive them to have.

Mental energy is our ability to focus related to our drive for self-expression.

Spiritual energy is the purpose we are grounded in and how much significance we feel.

To be fully engaged in our lives, we must be physically energized, mentally focused, emotionally connected, and spiritually aligned. Research in the science of energy management shows that people perform best when they move between using and renewing their energy across these four domains.[2] Knowing how to balance each kind of energy helps us know when we can perform at our best and when we need to take a break to recover, helping us build our emotional endurance.

Grow with the Flow

Think of the last time you were fully engaged in something you enjoyed *and* were good at. You may have even become so absorbed in this activity that hours flew by, feeling more like minutes. We see this with professional dancers, Olympic athletes, and even with young children engaging in pretend play. As spectators, we are drawn into the positive energy, enraptured in the moment along with the participants. But did you know that this state of flow also enhances your emotional endurance when you are fully engaged?

As an expert on the concept of *flow,* positive psychologist Mihaly Csikszentmihalyi studied how individuals engage in effortless action to create their best lives. He discovered that flow tends to occur when a person's skills are fully involved in overcoming a challenge that is *just* about manageable. Think of an Olympic gymnast focused on nailing her floor routine, a baseball player locked into the next pitch at the plate, or an artist carefully adding delicate brushstrokes to her masterpiece.

Notice that Csikszentmihalyi doesn't imply that what these people are doing is easy or comfortable. Rather, each individual experiences flow when they are involved in something that absorbs them fully while stretching their ability beyond their current limits.[3] These *optimal experiences* happen when individuals strike a balance between exercising their current abilities (skills) with a level of stretch (challenge).

When we show up and stretch ourselves in the face of obstacles instead of shrinking back, we become more capable the next time a challenge presents itself. "It is the full involvement of flow, rather than happiness, that makes for excellence in life," Csikszentmihalyi shares.[4] Driven by an enduring purpose to expand beyond our current comfort zone, we learn to use our energy to sharpen our skills while in a state of flow. Here, the age-old axiom "go with the flow" is more aptly rebranded "grow with the flow."

Track Your Energy

Your energy is what shapes the overall atmosphere. Whatever you feel internally gets expressed externally. Even when you face pressures and circumstances, when you take more control of your emotions, you can improve the quality of your energy. When you are fueled with positive energy, you become engaged and find your flow.

Take a regular "energy audit" by tracking how you feel compared to how engaged and productive you are throughout your day. Notice any overall trends in your daily energy, focus, and engagement. When are you the most present and motivated? What times of day require more breaks or periods of renewal before you reengage? It's also important to recognize any unusual external factors that may be affecting your energy levels.

Whatever you feel internally gets expressed externally.

When you recognize what parts of your regular routine are energizing and life-giving, you're able to intentionally plan when and how to do things best. Regularly checking in with yourself to track your energy highs and lows helps you identify your best (and worst) times to tackle a challenging task or have a hard conversation. This awareness helps you make space for your "big rocks" first when your energy is strongest so you can schedule draining tasks between them to recover faster. Managing your energy helps you renew your strength and build lasting emotional endurance.[5]

REFLECT + CONNECT

Take a regular "energy audit" over the next forty-eight hours using the following guidelines:

- Set periodic timers on your watch or phone at 9:00 a.m., 12:00 p.m., 3:00 p.m., 6:00 p.m., and 9:00 p.m. When the timer goes off, name how you feel along with any dips or spikes in your energy.

- Notice any overall trends in your daily energy, focus, and engagement. When are you the most present and motivated? What times of day require more breaks or periods of renewal before you reengage?
- What external factors are affecting your energy levels now? Notice this impact and how you can build in time for renewal to recharge.

SKILL 14

TRANSFORM STRESS INTO STRENGTH

Stepping out on stage with a brave smile, I felt a surge of anxiety juxtaposed with the excitement that I'd arrived at *this very moment*. As I stared out into the darkened auditorium into the audience, it was finally my turn to talk.

Nearly a decade before, I had walked onto a different stage to welcome 2,500 guests to TEDxSacramento when I was part of their production team. Now, just outside Orlando, I was standing on the famous red dot once again. But this time I was ready to deliver my first TEDx Talk.

As a professional speaker and leadership trainer who has presented to C-suite executives at global brands, I thought that this opportunity would feel more natural. But that day, my negative self-talk was in overdrive. Practicing what I teach, I quieted the inner chatter of my Saboteurs and started.

I began my talk with energy and passion, hoping to both

captivate and connect with the audience. And I *did* transfix the audience: by forgetting half of my second line and getting flustered. So I regained my composure and began again, finding my flow.

That afternoon on the stage, I modeled *exactly* what I was teaching: Just because you don't succeed the first time doesn't mean you've failed. It's okay to mess up, then recover and begin again.

Six months later, more than a million people around the world had listened to my TEDx Talk on how to start before you're ready. All because I had the courage to step up and turn my stress into strength.

What if we could learn to use stress to our advantage to enhance our performance? Together, let's explore the science behind our stress.

Lean into Your Stress

From a young age, we are taught that certain words are bad to say and we will get in trouble if we use them. As we grow up, one of the new dirty words we learn is *stress*. We don't like to admit when we're feeling stressed and often treat it like a personal failure or a weakness. In a culture that rewards hustle, productivity, and keeping it all together, saying you're stressed can feel like breaking an unspoken rule.

But at any given moment, most people can list at least three things that cause stress in their lives: finances and debt, career choices, extended family, challenging health situations, or future unknowns. Why are these things so stressful? And where does stress even come from?

The answers might surprise you.

"Stress is not the *circumstance*," shares Dr. Richard Swenson, the expert on margin. "It is our *response* to the circumstance."[1]

Let this sink in for a moment: The event itself does not cause stress. Our response is what generates our stress. Brené Brown upholds that "we feel stressed when we evaluate environmental demand as beyond our ability to cope successfully. . . . Our emotional reaction is more tied to our cognitive assessment of whether we can cope with the situation than to how our body is reacting."[2]

When we don't have the margin to meet the moment, we feel stressed.

In a nutshell, when we don't have the margin to meet the moment, we feel stressed.

But what if we lean into the feeling of being stretched beyond what we may feel capable of now? What if these are the moments that allow our capacity to increase in the present *and* for the future?

By expanding the range and depth of what you're able to hold, you can make your stress work for you. Rather than avoiding stressful situations, we find that research and practice show us that learning how to cope and overcome in the face of stress is what actually builds our capacity for emotional endurance.

Let's start by understanding the different types of stress and how they show up in our lives.

Make Your Stress Work for You

While teaching the Life Skills for College Students course at UCLA, my lecture room was filled with many high-performing student athletes who used stress to their advantage on the field or court. In my own life, I recognized that there were times when feeling a low level of stress actually increased my productivity and created positive outcomes. Curious about how stress and motivation were linked, I researched how overwhelm and anxiety show up in our bodies and impact our mindsets and behaviors.

While we often assume all stress is negative, there are actually three main types of stress humans experience:

1. **Distress:** Negative and destructive stress that occurs on a routine basis and is both internally and externally stimulated and reinforced.
2. **Hyperstress:** Excessive volume of negative stress that gets triggered in states of anxiety and overwhelm and can be chronic and debilitating.
3. **Eustress:** Positive stress that energizes and motivates us—but only to a certain point before it turns destructive.[3]

We tend to experience more stress when the stakes are higher and we care about something a great deal, which can move us into overdrive. "Stress and meaning are inextricably linked. You don't stress about things you don't care about, and you can't create a meaningful life without experiencing some stress," explains health psychologist Kelly McGonigal.[4] This is our *optimal zone* where stress is motivating as we engage in work that matters.

Research by psychologists Robert Yerkes and John Dillingham Dodson over a century ago found that this type of motivating eustress fuels our success—until it doesn't![5] Once we go over the stress tipping point, we experience negative impacts on performance, happiness, and well-being. The trick is to find—and stay—in this *optimal zone* with just enough positive stress (*eustress*) as a motivator to enhance your performance as you climb toward the peak.

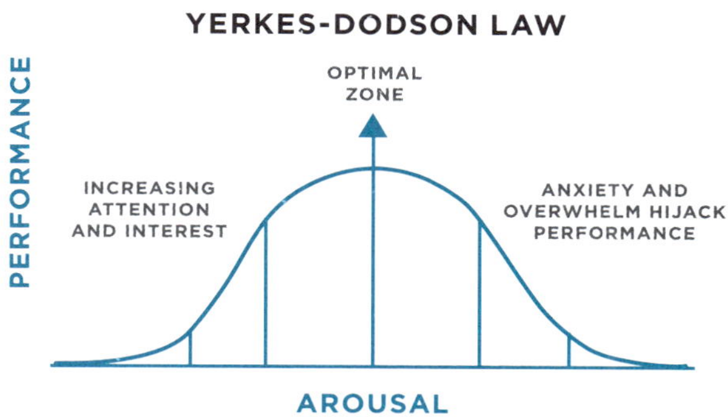

You can learn how to expand your stress threshold so you can handle more without tipping over the top. Doing so requires systematic exposure to *micro-stressors*: situations that are powerful enough to cause you stress without pushing you beyond what you're capable of managing. This makes the climb to the peak less steep as you extend the range of your *optimal zone*, increasing your emotional endurance.

YERKES-DODSON LAW

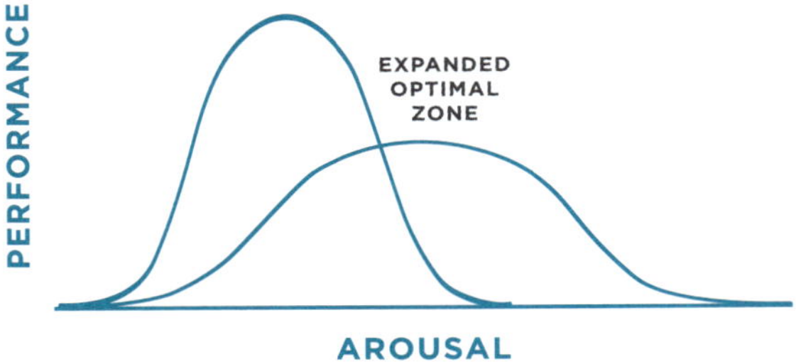

When we choose to engage in experiences that increase our stress and expand our capacity to handle what's hard, we develop emotional endurance for the long haul.

Understand Your Stress Response

Imagine being asked to travel hundreds of miles to one of the most dangerous places in the world to deliver a message no one really wants to hear. Would you go? Or would you ignore the request and maybe even run away?

That's exactly what happened to Jonah. He lived in Joppa on the western coast of Israel when God instructed him to travel 550 miles to modern-day Iraq to the city of Nineveh. Instead of following God's instructions, Jonah hopped on a boat to Tarshish—2,500 miles from Joppa—and ran from the Lord.[6]

Jonah was willing to travel more than four times the distance to *avoid* doing what God asked. Rather than engaging and embracing his stress, Jonah tried to escape.

But what if Jonah had leaned into his discomfort instead and used it to motivate his obedience?

Research has found that different ways of dealing with stress impact the outcomes we experience. "When you face difficulties head-on instead of trying to avoid or deny them, you build your resources for dealing with stressful experiences," McGonigal shares. "You become more confident in your ability to handle life's challenges."[7]

Powerhouse research team Alia Crum, Peter Salovey, and Shawn Achor studied the impact mindset has on a person's stress response in the face of challenges. They developed the Stress Mindset Measure that differentiates between two approaches to stress:

Mindset 1:
Stress is harmful (debilitating).

Mindset 2:
Stress is helpful (enhancing).[8]

Our mindset and approach to stress impact our behavior and performance. Individuals who view stress as *debilitating* tend either to over- or underreact to stress, assuming it will always negatively impact health, performance, and productivity. Like adopting a fixed mindset, these individuals avoid situations that seem too challenging or appear unfamiliar.

Our mindset and approach to stress impact our behavior and performance.

Approaching stress as *enhancing* helps improve one's performance, productivity, and overall health and well-being. This type of stress-related growth was found to fundamentally change individuals for the better, increasing their self-awareness, mental toughness, sense of mastery, relationship satisfaction, and meaningfulness in life.[9]

When we're experiencing overwhelm and anxiety in the form of *hyperstress*, we can choose either to *stew* or *renew* depending on our mindset.

STEW (*debilitating/fixed mindset*): Ruminate, process, blame, shame, guilt, deflect	**RENEW** (*enhancing/growth mindset*): Reset, release, forgive, recalibrate, recharge, restore

Stress shows up. By becoming more aware of the stress in your life and your response, you can reclaim more control over your mindset to improve your health and well-being. The next time you're feeling stressed or overwhelmed, try these five steps:

1. **Visualize your stress:** What color is it? If it were a type of weather, what would it be? How heavy is it? Take a moment to imagine how your stress is showing up to understand what is possible for you.
2. **Name how you're feeling:** When you give your emotions words, they have less immediate power. Name it to tame it!
3. **Notice where you care:** Since you naturally feel more stress about the things that matter most to you, this is a valuable opportunity to become aware of your core values at play.
4. **Refuel and refocus:** Stress naturally boosts your energy and increases your awareness by producing

more hormones that fuel your brain with blood and oxygen, helping you focus.

5. **Stay grounded in truth:** Remember these powerful spiritual reminders: Be anxious for nothing. God is sovereign and fully in control. God is never failing. God is never late. God will bring everything to fruition in His perfect timing for your good.[10]

As you learn to use stress as a strength, notice when your stress shows up either to enhance or diminish your energy as you continue developing your emotional endurance.

REFLECT + CONNECT

Think about your typical response to stress as you reflect on the following:

- Name a source of positive stress that motivates you. Where has this shown up recently?
- What effect does your stress have on your performance? Describe your optimal zone where you are the most productive.
- Consider your typical stress mindset. What opportunities are available to view stress as enhancing?

SKILL 15

CHOOSE YOUR LIFE CADENCE

Click. Click. Click. Click.

The metronome clicked steadily at 120 beats per minute as I tapped my foot in perfect rhythm. Holding my flute in position, I began playing along, matching the crescendo of the score as the music rose and swelled. When the song ended, I closed my eyes, absorbing the harmonies that echoed throughout the auditorium, reverberating off the walls and back into the audience.

I first came across the concept of cadence at a young age when I was starting to read and play music. In symphonic band, cadence was introduced to me as a rhythmic sequence where individual parts all work together to make a unified whole that is pleasing to listen to. Now a flutist for over three decades, I've learned to be attuned to the rhythm and flow of a piece of music, not only so I can know my part in the composition but also to discern how I can add value to the piece.

As we go about our days, we each follow a specific tempo that creates our life cadence. There are night owls and early risers. People who rush to get things done and others who take their time to ensure quality. Your daily rhythm shapes your life cadence, forming who you are and what others learn to expect of you. Similar to a symphony, our individual roles and identities in our families, friendships, schools, and workplaces shape our cadence based on the related culture, values, traditions, and routines we practice.

Your daily rhythm shapes your life cadence.

As I've studied cadence through these varied lenses, one central theme emerged: **We teach people how to treat us.**

The cadence we choose gives structure to our days so we become steady and reliable. When others know what to expect from us, our relationships are built on trust and accountability. These dependable life rhythms and relationships become even more essential in times of uncertainty, overwhelm, and chronic stress.

When you are out of cadence, your stress response typically defaults to undesirable behaviors that hijack your focus and influence. The two extremes tend to be *active behaviors* like striving, pushing, and hustling or *passive behaviors* such as avoiding, justifying, and procrastinating. Neither are appealing or fulfilling ways to live and lead. Instead, let's intentionally choose our cadence based on the rhythm of life we desire.

Create a Life Rhythm

You may be a solopreneur who is dreaming of finally launching your side hustle into a full-time business. Or a stay-at-home parent juggling multiple demands throughout your day. You might work in retail or food service, paying the bills while taking college classes. Or maybe you are one of the many people in between jobs and trying simply to make sense of life.

No matter your life stage or daily responsibilities, the rhythm you live by influences how you intentionally engage with your life, shaping your cadence. Just like selecting the perfect music to set the mood, we can choose what daily rhythm we follow. There are moments that call for fast action and decisive reasoning when the tempo picks up; other times require more thoughtful and strategic deliberation with an attitude of adagio, moving at a slower tempo.

Consider the concept of cadence as you reflect on your current pace of life:

- *Are there places where your life tempo is sluggish and you feel stuck?*
- *Are there times when your pulse is racing, leading to mounting stress, reactive decisions, and overwhelm?*

Whether you feel like you're living in fast-forward or slow motion, cadence impacts your energy to engage in what matters most to you. Consider how the daily rhythm you've chosen is serving you now or if changes are needed as you find the right tempo.

The rhythm you live by influences how you intentionally engage with your life, shaping your cadence.

Practice Energy Oscillation

Growing up playing competitive softball, I loved the feeling of fast action in the short sprints between bases. Yet I learned that this skill was the exact *opposite* technique required to complete a marathon. When aiming for longer distances, following a specific run-walk ratio allowed me to keep the pace and cross the finish line injury-free.

Similarly, we can practice energy *oscillation*: experiencing periods of stress and activity followed by periods of rest and recovery. You need both to move forward. Stress is what provides the stimulus for growth. Recovery is where the growth actually occurs.

Have you ever had a genius idea while you were in the shower or suddenly remembered something you'd been trying so hard to recall just as you were dozing off to sleep? The fixes to the problems we've been hustling to solve don't often come in the middle of the movement. Instead, when we allow our bodies and brains a chance to rest and recover, we are able to access more creative and innovative solutions.

> ***Stress is what provides the stimulus for growth. Recovery is where the growth actually occurs.***

I remember learning about the Pomodoro Technique in high school while studying for the SAT. This popular time-management approach separates focused work into intervals (twenty-five minutes) before taking a short break (five minutes) and then refocusing. After completing four cycles (thirty-minutes each over two hours), it's time to stop and recharge. Without pauses for rest, we are not as focused, energized, or productive. The system's creator, Francesco Cirillo, used a tomato-shaped kitchen timer that became the namesake of this productivity method: the Italian word for tomato, *pomodoro*.[1]

We learn something essential from the pause when choosing our cadence. It's the space between notes that is necessary to catch our breath before moving on to the next stanza. It's the wide margin on the pages in our lives that allows us to recapture our energy and make a bigger impact. It's a chance to dream, play, rest, and renew so we can keep going and move forward with emotional endurance.

Give Yourself Permission to Pause

We experience natural pauses in our daily lives: inhaling a deep breath, typing a comma, taking a nap, stopping at a red light, turning off our devices, or closing our eyes to tune out the visual noise.

Our pauses become powerful proclamations that we are finite beings who require rest. In fact, we were intentionally designed with this very concept in mind. Our all-powerful Creator demonstrated the importance of rest after He made the universe, Earth, and all that inhabits it in six days. God paused and rested: "Thus the heavens and the earth were completed in all their vast array. By the seventh day God had finished the work he had been doing. . . . Then God blessed the seventh day and made it holy, because on it **he rested from all the work of creating that he had done**" (Genesis 2:1–3 NIV, emphasis added).

Let's take a moment to consider this together: An eternal being who physically doesn't require rest to survive knew that pausing regularly to rest was *so essential* to His creation that He modeled it and also instructed us to set aside intentional, sanctified time weekly.[2] Observing the Sabbath has been a central spiritual practice for centuries and one I have kept since childhood. I often joke that our Creator knew He made people like me who literally won't stop unless we are commanded to do so!

Raising tiny humans and managing multiple businesses has energy costs. It's easy for me to try to get all the things done to feel a sense of productivity and accomplishment. I zip from thing to thing, checking off my mental boxes, often feeling overwhelmed and rushed. Years ago, I decided that I wanted to be at my best as the sun sets on Friday night. Instead of crashing into the end of the week and using the weekend to escape or recover, I desired to intentionally design a life where I felt energized and available, where I could be present and focused with my family, renewing our energy together on a weekly basis.

Through this shift, I've learned that when we intentionally design a life dynamic that values both hard work and purposeful rest with regular time to pause and ponder, something incredible happens. We create space for God to speak through us and use us for His glory, not just for the things we think we should do or the plans we made.

We put down the Sharpies we use to design our life agenda and trade them for plain old number two pencils (with big pink erasers). When we plan in pencil, we admit that we don't know it all and that God designed us for a purpose far bigger than we can create on our own as we become His masterpieces.[3]

Reconnecting with our daily rhythms on a deeper spiritual level creates a life cadence of action, pause, and reflection, including space to simply *not know*. To be astounded and amazed by what is possible instead of striving for answers and expertise. To be present and available as we live surrendered lives.

When we live with a balanced tempo, we invite in rest, recovery, and time to recharge alongside productivity and purpose. We set down our life-planning Sharpies and pick up our pencils instead, trusting that our works will be established.[4]

REFLECT + CONNECT

Considering your current life cadence, design your ideal weekly rhythm based on your natural energy cycles.

- If your life were a soundtrack, what tempo of music would be playing now?
- When and how are you regularly pausing to rest, renew, and recharge?
- What daily rhythm will bring you more fulfillment in your life? Notice anything you need to eliminate, adjust, or amplify.

PRINCIPLE SIX

PURPOSE TO PERSEVERE

When we are grounded in a purpose bigger than our current circumstances, we can activate an inner resolve to face whatever lies ahead. Individuals who possess grit fortified by faith are able to **persevere with purpose in the face of extreme challenges**, enhancing their emotional endurance. Using our natural strengths to drive our values forward, we find our flow and realign our expectations. Believing in this eternal purpose, we create a life of deep and abiding fulfillment as we leave a lasting legacy through our daily actions.

SKILL 16

DEFINE YOUR *WHY*

The college sophomore sitting in front of me stared back blankly as if I had spoken a foreign language.

"What are your core values?" I repeated, wondering if she simply hadn't heard me clearly the first time.

Tilting her head and squinting slightly, she finally responded in a timid voice, "What does *that* mean?"

"You know, the qualities you believe in and want to model in your life—the purpose behind your actions," I started to explain. "What character traits matter to you? What's your *why*?"

After pausing again, she quietly answered, "I've never really thought of that before."

When I worked in one of the largest residence halls at UCLA, it was my job to help develop students' leadership skills. I was also responsible for enforcing the rules. This particular sophomore had broken a housing policy and had been called in for remediation. Instead of highlighting her mistakes, I decided to take a different approach to help her refocus on the purpose behind her actions, starting with identifying her core values.

Over the next half hour, we discussed the cultural nuances that influenced her parents' expectations as the oldest daughter in an Asian American family. The student shared how she felt like she always had to be perfect and set a good example. So being called into my office was not only humiliating but downright shameful, causing her to shut down instead of show up with the integrity she was known for.

Taking in this new information, I helped her identify what mattered most to her: Responsibility, honesty, achievement, and kindness were at the top of her list. Then we went back to the situation that brought her to my office in the first place and identified where she had veered off course. With this approach, she clearly saw how her integrity had been weak in the moment. She needed a reset to realign with her core values. She needed to identify her *why*.

During our conversation, a new light shone in this young woman as she understood the importance of honoring her values through her everyday actions. When she left my office, I could see how our time together had allowed her to access something greater than simply having a corrective conversation. She had reclaimed her purpose to persevere.

Activate Your Values

Have you ever noticed how tall an oak tree grows yet doesn't break when strong winds blow? While invisible to the observer, the complex root system of this mighty oak supports the tree in the middle of the storm. These roots dig deep, creating a solid but invisible foundation as the tree matures over time. No matter what the oak faces, its roots hold it steady and allow it to withstand the weather.

Our values work the same way, grounding us deeply and holding us upright as we grow and develop throughout our lives, ready to face the storms ahead. The depth of our value structure determines how well we persevere when faced with challenges. Our values influence our behavior, guide our goals, and shape our identity. When we live in alignment with our values, we experience less friction and fewer negative emotions. We sway with the winds so our branches don't break.

Our values influence our behavior, guide our goals, and shape our identity.

Similar to roots of a tree, our values exist under the surface of our lives until we're asked about them in a job interview or a coaching session. Outside these experiences, many of us give our values little thought.

When did you first consider your core values? Formed through our culture, upbringing, and life experiences, our values shape what we believe and who we become, starting in childhood. Research on the formation of personal and individual differences shows how children's values are observable as early as five years old,[1] and how there is significant parent-child similarity in values and beliefs, especially in strongly religious families.[2] These value roots not only grow deep but also are broad as they span multiple generations.

Learning how to identify and model your core values through your daily actions and interactions is foundational to your character development. While there are many value-clarification exercises ranging from science-based assessments[3] to using simple values flash cards, the process is similar. Here are some prompts to help you start identifying your core values:

- *When were you the happiest or proudest in your life?*
- *Who do you admire and what qualities do they model?*
- *How do you want others to describe you?*

Review your responses and note any repeating themes. Then record words or phrases that point to your values. Write down as many as come to mind. This doesn't need to be an exhaustive list; just capture what you can. Now think of a place you pass by every day—a bathroom mirror, refrigerator door, or where you hang your keys—and post your core values where you will see them often. This visual reminder of your *why* becomes a daily reinforcer of the purpose behind how you want to live and who you are becoming.

Think about how you feel when you are living in alignment with what matters most in your life. With faith as your fuel, your values keep you moving toward your goals with enhanced emotional endurance. Living out our values becomes essential when our strength is tested beyond what we are capable of handling on our own.

Persevere for a Purpose

Less than a year after getting married in 1941, Viktor Frankl and his new wife, Tilly, along with Frankl's parents, were forced by Nazi soldiers to move to the Terezin ghetto just outside Prague. Within a few short months, Frankl watched his father die and then was moved to Auschwitz with the surviving members of his family. Before he turned forty, Frankl had spent a total of three years in four different concentration camps, losing his brother and mother at Auschwitz and his wife at Bergen-Belsen.

After the war ended, Frankl returned to Vienna alone, where he worked with resolve to reconstruct his life, starting with the manuscript that had been taken from him at Auschwitz. From his lived experience along with his professional practice as a psychiatrist, Frankl noticed how humans are motivated to find meaning in life through even the harshest of circumstances. "When we are no longer able to change a situation . . . we are challenged to change ourselves," Frankl wrote in his pivotal book *Man's Search for Meaning*.[4]

Frankl made it his life's mission to help individuals deal with and overcome existential struggles—such as isolation, meaninglessness, and grief—through the practice of *logotherapy*: Greek for "healing through meaning."[5] Frankl treated thousands of patients a year as they learned how to effectively cope with suffering. And his work didn't stop when he was taken into captivity with his family—it was fortified!

Frankl's story shows how **living on purpose—for a**

purpose—keeps you grounded in something bigger than your present circumstances. This approach to enduring present hardship for a future purpose allowed both Frankl and his patients to survive situations that would have ordinarily caused them to give up. The same meaning-making process allows us to endure hardship and persist in the face of setbacks because of our purpose to persevere.

Find Your *Why*

From summiting a tall mountain peak to laboring for hours to deliver a child, having a persistent purpose—a *why*—drives one's desire to keep going. People throughout history who were intrinsically motivated by a purpose bigger than themselves were able to overcome insurmountable circumstances. From the biblical stories we've explored together of Moses, David, Esther, Jesus, and Paul, we see how having a compelling *why* to face life's challenges fuels faith and persistence.

What's your *why*?

Consider the purpose that motivates you and encourages you to keep going, especially when it would be much easier not to. Maybe it's working out daily to maintain your health, showing up to your job as you provide for your family, or dedicating hours to a cause you believe in as you serve in your community. Our *why* is bigger than what we're experiencing in the moment: our career opportunities, children's development, health challenges, and even the greater goals we're working to achieve. While all of these things may matter a great deal now, your story was designed for an *eternal future* beyond your temporary circumstances and goals. As Proverbs 19:21 encourages, "Many are the plans in a person's heart, but it is the LORD's purpose that prevails" (NIV).

Don't lose sight of this everlasting focus: Your *why* must first be grounded in your identity as a cherished child of God.[6] Just as young children trust their parents to protect, guide, and love them, when we learn to fully rely on God and trust in His plan for our lives, we become open to the larger purpose He has in store for us. We are invited into a partnership with our Creator, recognizing that we cannot do anything fully on our own. Rather, it is the support and spiritual strength that are beyond our current capacity that empower our purpose to persevere.[7]

REFLECT + CONNECT

Reflecting on your *why*, use these questions to create your personal purpose statement:

- Who are you? Describe yourself based on the values and strengths that define and drive your life.
- What do you feel called to do with your life? Share where you feel led to serve and contribute your talents using your interests and passions.

- How will you improve the lives of others? Identify how your intentions will influence individuals and communities you're part of now.

SKILL 17

COMMIT TO GRIT

I watched the red tricycle tip over, almost as if it were happening in slow motion. The preschooler who had been flying by only seconds before now lay next to the trike on the playground, looking dazed. Before I could respond, he carefully stood up, reset the tricycle, and hopped back on. No tears, no complaints. Just resolve to get up and complete another loop around the yard.

Within minutes, a different student tripped and fell, quickly dissolving into a puddle of tears. Noting that the fall was minor and her reaction was more out of shock than pain, I observed the differences between the responses. I walked over to where she fell and saw that her big blue eyes were longing for comfort and attention.

As I sat with the tearful child, I watched the red tricycle make its way around to the spot where it had tipped over moments before. There was a sense of determination and strength in this first student's demeanor. Even before five years old, he had developed a drive to keep going and learned how to pick himself back up and continue on when things didn't go as planned. While the second student sought natural comfort and assurance that she would be okay, the first student had a different response to his fall: grit.

Grit is a personality trait of those who demonstrate passion and perseverance toward a goal despite being confronted by obstacles and distractions. From tenacious toddlers to audacious adults, people with grit don't quit. While resilient individuals bounce back from challenges quickly, those who possess grit persist for the long haul.

"Grit is more about stamina than intensity," psychologist Angela Duckworth contends. "Grit is about working on something you care about so much that you're willing to stay loyal to it."[1] By and large, those who possess grit are able to self-regulate and postpone their need for positive reinforcement or comfort while working diligently on a task. They are committed to showing up every day and putting in the effort. Their purpose to persevere against the odds is what drives their success.

You may have heard people say that there's no such thing as an overnight success. And that's true! We often see someone in the spotlight and think, *Of course they're successful. Look how much talent they have.* But as Duckworth examined the difference between talent and effort, she found that "if we overemphasize talent, we underemphasize everything else."[2] We overlook the years they've spent honing a skill. We overlook all the failures and setbacks they experienced on their way to the spotlight, unaware of the true investment of money, time, and sacrifice along their road to success.

Performing well at something requires more than just possessing a skill and replicating it over and over again. Building on what we've learned about strengths development and growth mindset, our natural talent is only a starting place—not the finish line. We still have to run the race and keep the pace. We have to exert continual effort and stay committed to the goal, even—and especially—when it gets hard.

Realign Your Expectations

"Plan the event, not the outcome."

This advice from my college professor still sticks with me to this day, especially when the end results don't align with my expectations. While having high standards can drive performance as we go after our goals with grit, these same expectations can also hijack our sense of fulfillment when they don't match reality.

The father of American psychology, William James, determined that a person's sense of self-worth depends largely on their ratio of expectations to successes. James developed the following equation to determine how someone feels about themselves based on what they experience:

Let's look at all three elements of this equation.

$$\text{Self-esteem} = \frac{\text{Stress}}{\text{Pretentions}}$$

1. **Self-esteem:** Confidence in one's own worth, abilities, or morals
2. **Success:** Our accomplishments, or how well we attain our achievements
3. **Pretension:** Our intentions or aspirations for ourselves[3]

As a self-proclaimed "recovering perfectionist," I appreciate a well-executed plan that goes smoothly. I also recognize that despite my best efforts, many things can go wrong as I'm executing that plan. In those moments, I have a choice: I can abandon my plan and quit, or I can continue and see what's possible. That's where grit doubles down: In the places and spaces we're frustrated, stuck, disappointed, or heartbroken, grit helps us bounce back and choose to keep going.

From cooking to parenting, there is no perfect recipe for success, just some good instructions and our investment of energy, effort, and engagement. Learning how to realign our expectations to something attainable helps us gain a sense of success and accomplishment, boosting our self-esteem. We take stock in what we've already done rather than become stuck on the unchecked boxes or unanswered prayers. We recommit to grit as we celebrate our small wins.

Reframe Your "To-Dos" as "Ta-Das"

As someone who loves making and checking off lists, I often feel discouraged and even disappointed when I don't make as much progress on my to-do list as I had hoped. It's so easy to focus on all the things I *haven't done yet* instead of celebrating what progress is made or tasks are complete.

A few years ago, I began creating *a different kind of list* that increased my productivity and produced a sense of positive accomplishment. Setting aside intentional time before bed, I reflect on my day and capture all of my "ta-das": when I made progress, completed something, or simply felt good about how I spent my time. Writing down my daily accomplishments renews my energy as I refocus on the goals ahead rather than criticize what still needs to be done. I find peace in the "not yet" spaces instead of staying stuck in FOMO or resentment.

The daily practice of creating my "ta-da" list helped me stop judging all the unchecked boxes on my to-do list so I could consider what I was proud to accomplish each day. There are even times throughout my day when I catch myself thinking or even saying "ta-da" (complete with jazz hands, of course!) when I finish something or make progress on a goal. These micro-celebrations are important reminders that our efforts matter as we cheer on ourselves and others with genuine acknowledgment.

Honor the process of learning and growth by taking stock of your successes as you fuel your fulfillment.

Creating my "ta-da" list inspires me to keep moving forward with grit toward purposeful action. When you commit to growing your grit, you can honor the process of learning and growth by taking stock of your successes as you fuel your fulfillment.

Run the Best You Can

"Dad, what are all of those?" asked my son Caleb, gesturing to the shiny trophies lining our fireplace mantel.

"Those are for the races I won in high school and college," Joel shared. "But the best race I ever ran was when I came in second. There is no trophy for that."

This unexpected answer stopped me in my tracks.

Since Joel has always been a highly competitive runner, his confession seemed inaccurate. *Second place? Really?* I thought in disbelief.

I paused next to our children, eager for his explanation, but Caleb beat me to the question. "Why second, Dad?"

Joel smiled and shared a lesson that I still regularly apply in my life.

"I ran that race with everything I had," he explained. "And coming in second was the best I could do given the conditions and my competitors. So I know I did my absolute best, even if I didn't win the race or get a trophy."

How often do we look at where we've landed and judge what we *didn't achieve* instead of celebrating our smaller wins?

Coming in second for Joel in that race was a bigger deal than winning because he knew he had pushed himself to his maximum effort and felt a sense of pride and accomplishment. He had locked into a flow state and expanded his limits through his physical, mental, and emotional endurance. Through his grit, he activated a purpose to run the race in front of him that fueled his perseverance, despite the outcome.

When I think about the lesson I learned from Joel that day, I also think about the way the Bible uses running as a metaphor for living our lives with spiritual discipline:

> Don't you know that in a race all the runners compete, but only one wins the prize? So then, run to win! Now every athlete in training submits himself to strict discipline, and he does it just to win a laurel wreath that will soon wither away. But we do it to win a crown that will last forever. (1 Corinthians 9:24–25 CJB)

As we focus on achieving our goals in a way that aligns with our values, our grit propels us forward. The Bible also encourages our grit with a deeper spiritual purpose, saying, "Blessed is the one who perseveres under trial because, having stood the test, that person will receive the crown of life that the Lord has promised to those who love him" (James 1:12 NIV). This eternal reward is bigger than any temporary achievement or trophy. It's a lasting crown that will not perish.

How will you choose to run?

REFLECT + CONNECT

Reflect on ways your grit already is propelling your purpose.

- Think back to a time when you kept going, despite the circumstances. What did this experience teach you?
- Examine your current expectations. How do they align with your benchmarks for success?
- Create your own daily "ta-da" list. What are your small wins as well as any "not yet" spaces for future growth?

SKILL 18

FUEL YOUR FULFILLMENT

Astronaut! Ballerina! Firefighter! Superhero!

I looked back at the excited faces of the preschoolers I was teaching as they responded eagerly to my question: "What do you want to do when you grow up?" Their faces lit up as they described jobs that reflected their current interests. But I knew in the years ahead their responses would shift.

Working in college student services showed me that the career you might have in two decades may not even exist now. While we can be thankful for the jobs that provide for our needs, many of us may feel stuck in a career path our younger self chose from a list of college majors or a job we fell into and just kept going. Others feel unsure about what more may be out there and if fulfillment is truly possible.

As I collaborate with clients around the world, I've started putting a fresh spin on this familiar question in our coaching sessions by asking them: "Who do you want *to be* when you grow up?" No matter who I ask this question to, this reframe gets respondents thinking deeper about the qualities they desire to cultivate throughout their lives. Why? I think because the question emphasizes how your *being* fuels your *doing*, and not the other way around.

I've used this coaching method to help thousands of people intentionally design lives that reflect their greatest priorities as they live with purpose. Posing this question to everyone from college freshmen to executive leaders nearing retirement, I found that all their responses showcased one common theme: Each of us wants to leave behind a legacy we can be proud of. Creating your legacy is not about the job you aspire to have but the life you desire to live.

Creating your legacy is not about the job you aspire to have but the life you desire to live.

Visualize Your Future

When was the last time you reflected on how you're living right now? In her poem "The Summer Day," American poet Mary Oliver asked this question a different way: "Tell me, what is it you plan to do with your one wild and precious life?"[1]

Together we've explored everything from identifying our natural strengths and core values to managing our energy and stress responses as we redefine success. Now, let's integrate these concepts as we create life legacies that fuel our fulfillment.

I often use a "future self" visualization exercise in my professional practice as a way to align current actions with underlying intentions. Research shows that visualization can boost our expectations and strengthen the belief that our efforts will lead to success.[2] When we can clearly see what we desire, we can take intentional steps toward the future we aspire to create.

I invite you to take out something to write with, get comfortable, and spend a few minutes traveling with me into your future.

Imagine you've traveled forward twenty years and you're attending a gala hosted in your honor. Everyone who has been important in your life is filling the banquet hall. When you arrive, the room quiets to a cheerful lull and then erupts into applause as you take a seat in an inviting armchair next to the podium. One by one, people who have played a significant role in your life take the stage and begin to share stories highlighting the difference you have made. From childhood friends and family members to professional colleagues, their narratives weave together to showcase your life's legacy. As the night comes to an end, you say your goodbyes and return home. Drifting off to sleep and waking back up in the present day, you are now fully aware of the impact you have made.

As we end this visualization exercise, take a moment to capture your reflections:

- *What did you experience?*
- *How did you feel seeing your "future self"?*
- *Was there anything that surprised you?*
- *How will this information shape your life now?*

For some, this exercise is eye-opening, showcasing how the choices they are making now will shape their future. Others may respond more critically if they don't feel like they have contributed enough or believe they're not on the right path. Instead of looking at what hasn't happened yet or what you fear may not occur, I invite you to use this exercise to consider what your version of a fulfilled life looks and feels like as you create your legacy through intentional daily actions.

It's important to note that leaving a legacy you're proud of doesn't require putting forth some grand gesture or becoming someone who's internationally recognized. You don't need to be a famous influencer or win a big award to make a difference. Rather, our legacies are created through the simple, daily practices of showing up for people and doing what we can with the time and resources available to us:

- *Investing time with your young children and grandchildren*
- *Mentoring a colleague at work*
- *Grocery shopping for an elderly neighbor*
- *Volunteering for a cause you care about*

- *Planting a backyard garden*
- *Creating something that improves the lives of others*

Consider the people, places, and spaces you are impacting on a regular basis. Notice the difference you're making, paying attention to the smiles, hugs, and even the silent nods of gratitude that often go unspoken. All of these moments create a fulfilling life through your actions and interactions, shaping what you are known for and who you are becoming. By showing up and living with purpose, you are creating your legacy each day.

Embrace Areté

What does it mean to truly *live*, and live *well*?

More than two thousand years ago, Greek philosopher Aristotle lectured his pupils on the idea of *eudaimonia*, or one's human flourishing achieved through developing virtuous character.[3] A related Greek concept is *areté*, which describes the path of seeking excellence and developing the full realization of one's potential. The idea is first referenced in Homer's *Odyssey* through the character of Arete, queen of the Phaeacians, who displays intelligence, prowess, and moral goodness, playing a pivotal role in Odysseus's journey home.[4]

We can embody this notion of wholehearted fullness, sharing truth, light, and hope. Our calling from above is clear: We are to become like our Father. Matthew 5:48 says, "Therefore you shall be perfect, just as your Father in heaven is perfect" (NKJV).

That sounds daunting, right? We know we will never be perfect like God in this human life. But let's take a closer look at the meaning of this verse, because there's more we can learn when we search under the surface.

The Greek word for "perfect" described in this verse is *teleios*, which means "complete," indicating a finished product.[5] Now notice Matthew's instructions of "you *shall* be." This implies that we aren't complete *yet*. We're in a process of becoming complete, which is a comforting reminder since we are still messy, incredible works in progress. In order to become perfect and embrace areté, we need to exemplify Jesus through our everyday actions as we learn, grow, and overcome.

Create Your Legacy

Every year on my birthday, I do two things: First, I write a letter to myself one year from today on a pretty card that I will open next year on my birthday. Then, I open the card I wrote the year before. As I'm writing, I think about how the last year has gone, taking stock of the progress I made and the goals I achieved, noting any life milestones or significant lessons learned. Next, I make a list of aspirations, hopes, and dreams for the year ahead. Then I seal the letter and save it until my next birthday.

Opening the card I had written in early March 2020, just days before finding out I was pregnant with our daughter, Eden Rose, I wept tears of gratitude for the baby I now held and the hard year we had endured. Despite the challenges we faced, I remained faithful in the middle of a wilderness season, when the answers I so desperately prayed for were absent. I made meals for friends who had new babies. I folded endless loads of laundry. I wrote thank-you cards and checked in on sick loved ones. I ran two businesses and worked hard to support our family. I did what I could with what I had. And through it all, I continued showing up and trusting that God was working it all out for His greater good.

We don't have time machines. In the middle of the mess, we often cannot see the pieces that are being put in place. Through choosing to stay faithful and focused on the purpose driving our actions, we create legacies and fulfilling lives, even when we're still in a wilderness season or a waiting place. We create our lifelong legacies through our daily actions: by showing up and doing the work in front of us with an obedient spirit while believing in a greater purpose yet to come.

We're invited to lay down the heavy yoke we're trying to shoulder on our own and embrace the light load we are promised when we rest and abide in Christ.[6] Together we can carry each other's burdens as we illuminate our collective gifts.[7] We can trust that the good work that has been started in us now will be fulfilled.[8] By persevering on purpose for an eternal purpose, we'll leave a lasting legacy with our emotional endurance.

We create our lifelong legacies through our daily actions.

REFLECT + CONNECT

Carve out some time in the next twenty-four hours to write a letter to your "future self" one year from today. (You don't have to wait until it's your birthday!)

- What do you desire to create, cultivate, and construct?
- What do you hope to have released, retired, or removed from your life?
- When you're done writing, notice how you feel. What legacy are you creating now?

Put your letter somewhere for safekeeping and set a reminder to open it a year from today. You can also adopt my practice of writing a new letter *before* opening the other one.

MOVING FORWARD

The multitudes looked west toward the overflowing river. During this harvest season, the air felt rich with the promise of a long-awaited reward that lay beyond the horizon. They just had to cross the water to claim it. It had been only a month since Moses passed on, leaving Joshua in charge to lead the Israelites onward. When they finally reached the Plains of Moab with the promised land in sight, they stood at the east bank of the Jordan River awaiting instruction.[1]

Forty years of wilderness wandering had led them to this exact moment.

Now what?

You may be here, too, standing at the edge of a long-awaited goal or future dream that feels so close yet just out of reach. The desire to keep going is strong, yet uncertainty is all you see; the water you're facing is deep and the way forward isn't clear. Then the familiar stream of questions begins to bubble up from under the surface:

> *Do I have what it takes?*
> *Am I strong enough?*
> *Can I make it?*

I'm here to remind you that yes—yes you can. And you will. But *not* by standing still.

Together we've explored some core concepts that address these doubts head-on. From shifting your mindset, to tracking your energy and activating your strengths, you've practiced new skills to help expand your capacity for emotional endurance. And now you're here, on the brink of your own crossing.

Are you ready to move forward and claim the promises God has in store for you? It's time to step out and see what's possible on the other side of the shore.

Step Out and Cross Over

The Jordan River marked the final boundary between all the wandering and the enduring promise for the people of Israel. The water was deep, and there were still miles to go. But this wasn't the first time many of these weary travelers faced an impassable obstacle. Joshua and Caleb had been there when they fled Egypt and crossed the Red Sea walking through on dry land.[2] After forty years of wandering, the older generation of Israelites had perished, and the new generation knew only the wilderness and the miracles God had performed as He tested and refined their faith, preparing them for this very moment.

After decades of following in faith, the Israelites eagerly stood awaiting the fulfillment of all their hard work. God instructed Joshua to tell the priests carrying the sacred ark of the covenant that, once they reached the water's edge, they should go stand in the river.[3] The water had not moved before they took their first step in and the banks were overflowing. They acted on faith first and watched God do the rest. Just as before, when they were fleeing the Egyptians, God parted the water, and they crossed safely on dry ground into the promised land.

Imagine what would be possible if you were willing to take that first step forward in faith before you felt *ready*, walking into the new territory God has prepared for you. Even when—and especially when—the current conditions of your life aren't perfect, you're still called to move.

What bold steps of faith are you willing to take?
What are you ready to lay down and release?
What would be possible then?

Find Strength in Surrender

In our culture it is counterintuitive to find strength in surrender. But when we are emotionally and physically weak, we are more able to become spiritually strong. When God said, "My grace is sufficient for you, for my power is made perfect in weakness," the apostle Paul said, "I will boast all the more gladly about my weaknesses, so that Christ's power may rest on me. That is why, for Christ's sake, I delight in weaknesses, in insults, in hardships, in persecutions, in difficulties. **For when I am weak, then I am strong**" (2 Corinthians 12:9–10 NIV, emphasis added).

This is the precious space that God can use to grow us beyond what we're capable of on our own, and the only way we are able to develop emotional endurance. Living a surrendered life is the strongest thing we can do in our broken world.

When life gets hard, we can allow our hearts to remain soft and teachable as we submit to a higher purpose. We have to be willing to surrender and take the first step off the shore to discover the new territory God has in store for us.

Living a surrendered life is the strongest thing we can do in our broken world.

When we accept feeling lost, stuck, or behind, we build our capacity for what's *next*. We listen. We pause. We approach the unexpected situation as a chance to learn. We continue refining our skills so we have a shot at the next big promotion or opportunity. We become solution seekers driven by the possibility of what's ahead. We access more hope with our willpower and our waypower.[4] We discover more energy to engage. We move forward into the promise of a future far greater than anything we could ever imagine on our own, trusting that God "has made everything beautiful in its time. He has also set eternity in the human heart; yet no one can fathom what God has done from beginning to end" (Ecclesiastes 3:11 NIV).

Trust the Process

As we reach the end of our journey together, I invite you to remember that growing your capacity for emotional endurance is both a daily and a lifelong process. While many of these skills we've learned together can be practiced in the present, developing your emotional endurance as a lasting resource requires sustained effort.

You haven't arrived yet. And that's okay.

You're a beautiful, imperfect work in progress on your way to self-mastery.

Some days you'll do incredible things.

And some days (or weeks) you may feel stuck or even slide backward.

That's part of the human experience.

Your goals may change or take on a new form altogether.

What matters is that you stick with it and never give up—remembering that you have permission to pause, rest, reflect, and reboot.

God does not promise us easy. But He *does* promise to be with us through the hard. It's your emotional endurance that allows you to continue on, knowing that you're never alone. As you slow down and surrender, you allow the next steps to unfold in God's perfect timing.

God does not promise us easy. But He does *promise to be with us through the hard.*

My hope is that through the pages of this book, you have gained and refined a set of skills that help you along your journey. Most importantly, I pray that you have deepened your faith, hope, and trust in the very Creator who designed you with the capacity to grow, develop, change, create, and leave a lasting legacy with your life.

Don't ever limit what God can do through your one incredible life.

Invite Him into it all, allowing God to guide and shape your story for His eternal glory.

Press on.

Keep going.

Live and lead with the emotional endurance you were designed to embody.

While it is bound to have its challenges, I promise it will be worth it.

> Brothers and sisters, I do not consider myself yet to have taken hold of it. But one thing I do: Forgetting what is behind and straining toward what is ahead, I press on toward the goal to win the prize for which God has called me heavenward in Christ Jesus.
>
> **PHILIPPIANS 3:13–14 NIV**

NOTES

The Need for Emotional Endurance

1. Amit Goldenburg, David Garcia, Eran Halperin, Jamil Zaki, Danyang Kong, Golijeh Golarai et al., "Beyond Emotional Similarity: The Role of Situation-Specific Motives," *Journal of Experimental Psychology: General* 149, no. 1 (2020): 138–59, https://psycnet.apa.org/record/2019-32092-001?doi=1.
2. Genesis 1:27; Deuteronomy 30:19; Ecclesiastes 7:29.
3. Romans 5:3–4.
4. Susan Folkman, "Positive Psychological States and Coping with Severe Stress," *Social Science & Medicine* 45, no. 8 (1997): 1207–21, https://doi.org/10.1016/S0277-9536(97)00040-3.

Skill 1: Name It to Tame It

1. Alan S. Cowen and Dacher Keltner, "Self-Report Captures 27 Distinct Categories of Emotion Bridged by Continuous Gradients," *PNAS* 114, no. 38 (2017): E7900–E7909, https://doi.org/10.1073/pnas.1702247114.
2. James J. Gross, "Emotion Regulation: Affective, Cognitive, and Social Consequences," *Psychophysiology* 39, no. 3 (2002): 281–91, https://doi.org/10.1017/S0048577201393198.
3. Genesis 1:27; Romans 8:28.
4. Philippians 4:8.

Skill 2: Learn to Discern

1. Parker J. Palmer, *Let Your Life Speak: Listening for the Voice of Vocation* (Jossey-Bass, 2000), 55.
2. Proverbs 3:5–6.
3. Cleere Cherry Reaves, *Focus: How One Word a Week Will Transform Your Life* (DaySpring, 2020), 177.
4. P. C. Wason and J.ST.B.T. Evans, "Dual Processes in Reasoning?," *Cognition* 3, no. 2 (1974–1975): 141–54, https://doi.org/10.1016/0010-0277(74)90017-1.
5. Daniel Kahneman, "A Perspective on Judgement and Choice: Mapping Bounded Rationality," *American Psychologist* 58, no. 9 (2003): 697–720, http://www2.econ.iastate.edu/tesfatsi/JudgementAndChoice.MappingBoundedRationality.DKahneman2003.pdf.
6. Proverbs 16:3.

Skill 3: Fail Forward in Your Strengths

1. Romans 12:6–8.
2. Ryan M. Niemiec, "Finding the Golden Mean: The Overuse, Underuse, and Optimal Use of Character Strengths," *Counselling Psychology Quarterly*, 32, nos. 3–4 (2019): 453-71, https://doi.org/10.1080/09515070.2019.1617674.
3. Hebrews 13:5.
4. 2 Corinthians 12:10.
5. Philippians 4:13.

Skill 4: Face the Unknown with Faith

1. J. A. Easterbrook, "The Effect of Emotion on Cue Utilization and the Organization of Behavior," *Psychological Review* 66, no. 3 (1959): 183–201, https://doi.org/10.1037/h0047707.
2. Sarah Sperber, "Fight or Flight Response: Definition,

Symptoms, and Examples," Berkeley Well-Being Institute, https://www.berkeleywellbeing.com/fight-or-flight.html.
3. "Resilience," American Psychological Association, https://www.apa.org/topics/resilience.
4. Dr. Zelana Montminy, *21 Days to Resilience: How to Transcend the Daily Grind, Deal with the Tough Stuff, and Discover Your Strongest Self* (HarperOne, 2016), 4.
5. Ilona Boniwell and Aneta D. Tunariu, *Positive Psychology: Theory, Research and Applications*, 2nd ed. (Open University Press, 2019), 134.
6. John 15:19–20; 1 Peter 4:12–13.
7. Mark 10:29–30.
8. John 10:10.
9. Matthew 5:10–12.

Skill 5: Shift Your Perspective

1. Norton Juster, *The Phantom Tollbooth* (Yearling, 1988), 107–8.
2. Arien Mack and Irvin Rock, "Inattentional Blindness: Perception Without Attention," in *Visual Attention*, ed. Richard D. Wright (Oxford University Press, 1998), 55–76, https://doi.org/10.1080/07303084.2014.988373.
3. Barbara L. Fredrickson, "The Broaden-and-Build Theory of Positive Emotions," *Philosophical Transactions of the Royal Society of London, Series B, Biological Sciences* 359, no. 1449 (2004): 1367–77, https://doi.org/10.1098/rstb.2004.1512.
4. Barbara L. Fredrickson, "Cultivating Positive Emotions to Optimize Health and Well-Being," *Prevention & Treatment* 3, no. 1 (2000): Article 1, https://psycnet.apa.org/doi/10.1037/1522-3736.3.1.31a.
5. Romans 15:13; Isaiah 40:31.
6. 1 Samuel 17:40.

7. 1 Samuel 25:2–43.
8. John 12:9.

Skill 6: Clarify Your Core Drivers

1. Amanda Reill, "A Simple Way to Make Better Decisions," *Harvard Business Review*, December 5, 2023, https://hbr.org/2023/12/a-simple-way-to-make-better-decisions.
2. Andrew Alstot and Crystal Alsot, "Behavior Management: Examining the Functions of Behavior," *Journal of Physical Education, Recreation & Dance* 86, no. 2 (2015): 22–28, https://doi.org/10.1080/07303084.2014.988373.
3. Kurt Lewin, *Field Theory in Social Science: Selected Theoretical Papers* (Harper and Row, 1951), 224.
4. J. W. Moore, "What Is the Sense of Agency and Why Does It Matter?" *Frontiers in Psychology* 7 (2016): 1272, https://doi.org/10.3389/fpsyg.2016.01272.
5. Herbert M. Lefcourt, "Locus of Control," in *Measures of Personality and Social Psychological Attitudes*, eds. John P. Robinson, Philip R. Shaver, and Lawrence S. Wrightsman, vol. 1, *Measures of Social Psychological Attitudes* (Academic Press, 1991), 413–99, https://doi.org/10.1016/B978-0-12-590241-0.50013-7.
6. Proverbs 16:9.
7. 2 Timothy 1:7.
8. Romans 12:2.

Skill 7: Wait, Wander, and Wonder

1. John 9:1–7.
2. Mark 5:25–29.
3. Matthew 8:1–3.

4. James 1:2–4.
5. C. R. Snyder, *The Psychology of Hope: You Can Get There from Here* (Free Press, 1994), 10.
6. Matthew 3:13–17.
7. Deuteronomy 31:1–3.
8. Deuteronomy 31:9.
9. Hebrews 5:9; 9:12.

Skill 8: Create Margin to Recover

1. Richard A. Swenson, *Margin: Restoring Emotional, Physical, Financial, and Time Reserves to Overloaded Lives* (NavPress, 2004), 69.
2. Swenson, *Margin*, 70.
3. Swenson, *Margin*, 25.
4. Emily P. Freeman, host, *The Next Right Thing*, podcast, episode 87, "Create Space," June 18, 2019, https://emilypfreeman.com/podcast/87/, at 10:16.
5. Leviticus 19:9–10; 23:22; 25:2; Exodus 23:10–11.
6. Ecclesiastes 3:1–11.
7. Psalm 46:10; John 15:4–9.
8. Matthew 14:23; Mark 6:46–47; Luke 6:12; John 6:15.

Skill 9: Envision Your Future

1. Laura A. King, "The Health Benefits of Writing About Life Goals," *Personality and Social Psychology Bulletin* 27, no. 7 (2001): 798–800, https://doi.org/10.1177/0146167201277003.
2. Deb Dana, *The Polyvagal Theory in Therapy: Engaging the Rhythm of Regulation* (W. W. Norton, 2018).
3. 2 Peter 3:8–9.
4. Revelation 21:1–4.

Skill 10: Say Goodbye to Someday

1. Michele DeMarco, "The Art and Science of Courage," Medium, February 10, 2021, https://michelejdemarco.medium.com/the-art-and-science-of-courage-abfec1a6a064.
2. Exodus 3:1–3.
3. 1 Samuel 17:45–50.
4. Daniel 6:16–17.
5. Esther 4:14–16.
6. Bruce Goldman, "Scientists Find Fear, Courage Switches in Brain," Stanford School of Medicine, May 2, 2018, https://med.stanford.edu/news/all-news/2018/05/scientists-find-fear-courage-switches-in-brain.html.
7. Uri Nili et al., "Fear Thou Not: Activity of Frontal and Temporal Circuits in Moments of Real-Life Courage," *Neuron* 66, no. 6 (2010): 949–62, https://doi.org/10.1016/j.neuron.2010.06.009.
8. Kelly McGonigal, "How to Transform Stress into Courage and Connection," *Greater Good*, May 13, 2015, https://greatergood.berkeley.edu/article/item/how_to_transform_stress_courage_connection.
9. Brené Brown, *Daring Greatly: How the Courage to Be Vulnerable Transforms the Way We Live, Love, Parent, and Lead* (Avery, 2015), 30.
10. James 1:19–22.

Skill 11: Manage Your Mindset

1. Carol S. Dweck, *Mindset: The New Psychology of Success* (Ballentine Books, 2006), 46.
2. Dweck, *Mindset*, 6–7.
3. Melissa De Witte, "Stanford Scholar Applies a Norwegian Mindset About Winter to a COVID-19 World," Stanford Report,

December 18, 2020, https://news.stanford.edu/stories/2020/12/norwegian-mindset-winter-might-help-covid-19-world.

4. De Witte, "Standford Scholar Applies a Norwegian Mindset."
5. 1 Peter 2:22; Matthew 26:15; 27:31; 28:1–10.
6. Deuteronomy 31:8.

Skill 12: Expand Your Comfort Zone

1. 1 Corinthians 1:9; 2 Timothy 1:9.
2. Linda Adams, "Learning a New Skill Is Easier Said than Done," Gordon Training International, accessed November 12, 2025, https://www.gordontraining.com/free-workplace-articles/learning-a-new-skill-is-easier-said-than-done/.
3. Exodus 16:2–3.
4. Numbers 11:1–15.
5. Exodus 13:21–22.

Skill 13: Enhance Your Energy

1. Jim Loehr and Tony Schwartz, *The Power of Full Engagement: Managing Energy, Not Time, Is the Key to High Performance and Personal Renewal* (Free Press, 2003), 9.
2. Loehr and Schwartz, *The Power of Full Engagement*, 5, 46.
3. Mihaly Csikszentmihalyi, *Finding Flow: The Psychology of Engagement with Everyday Life* (Basic Books, 1997), 29–30.
4. Csikszentmihalyi, *Finding Flow*, 32.
5. Isaiah 40:31.

Skill 14: Transform Stress into Strength

1. Richard A. Swenson, *Margin: Restoring Emotional, Physical, Financial, and Time Reserves to Overloaded Lives* (NavPress, 2004), 44.

2. Brené Brown, *Atlas of the Heart: Mapping Meaningful Connection and the Language of Human Experience* (Random House, 2021), 5–6.
3. Swenson, *Margin*, 44–45.
4. Kelly McGonigal, *The Upside of Stress: Why Stress Is Good for You, and How to Get Good at It* (Avery, 2015), xxii.
5. Robert M. Yerkes and John D. Dodson, "The Relation of Strength of Stimulus to Rapidity of Habit-Formation," *Journal of Comparative Neurology & Psychology* 18, no. 5 (1908): 459-82, https://doi.org/10.1002/cne.920180503.
6. Jonah 1:1–3.
7. McGonigal, *Upside of Stress*, 18.
8. Alia J. Crum, Peter Salovey, and Shawn Achor, "Rethinking Stress: The Role of Mindsets in Determining the Stress Response," *Journal of Personality and Social Psychology* 104, no. 4 (2013): 716–33, https://psycnet.apa.org/doi/10.1037/a0031201.
9. Crystal L. Park and Vicki S. Helgeson, "Introduction to the Special Section: Growth Following Highly Stressful Life Events—Current Status and Future Directions," *Journal of Consulting and Clinical Psychology* 74, no. 5 (2006): 791–96, https://psycnet.apa.org/doi/10.1037/0022-006X.74.5.791.
10. Philippians 4:6–7; Colossians 1:16–17; Zephaniah 3:5; 2 Peter 3:9; Romans 8:28.

Skill 15: Choose Your Life Cadence

1. Francesco Cirillo, *The Pomodoro Technique: The Acclaimed Time-Management System That Has Transformed How We Work* (Crown Currency, 2018), 11.
2. Exodus 20:8–11.

3. Ephesians 2:10.
4. Proverbs 16:3.

Skill 16: Define Your Why

1. Anni Tamm and Tiia Tulviste, "Children's Values in Early Childhood: Age Differences in Structure and Priorities," *Personality and Individual Differences* 184, no. 3 (2022): 111–96, https://doi.org/10.1016/j.paid.2021.111196.
2. Alan Cooperman, "Most U.S. Parents Pass Along Their Religion and Politics to Their Children," Pew Research Center, May 10, 2023, https://www.pewresearch.org/short-reads/2023/05/10/most-us-parents-pass-along-their-religion-and-politics-to-their-children/.
3. "Discover Your Strengths," VIA Institute on Character, accessed September 15, 2025, https://www.viacharacter.org.
4. Viktor E. Frankl, *Man's Search for Meaning: An Introduction to Logotherapy*, 4th ed., trans. Ilse Lasch (Beacon Press, 1992), 105.
5. "Who Was Viktor Frankl?," The Viktor E. Frankl Institute of America, accessed September 15, 2025, https://viktorfranklamerica.com/viktor-frankl-bio/.
6. 1 John 3:2.
7. 1 Corinthians 10:13.

Skill 17: Commit to Grit

1. Angela Duckworth, *Grit: The Power of Passion and Perseverance* (Scribner, 2016), 53–54.
2. Duckworth, *Grit*, 35.
3. William James, *The Principles of Psychology*, vol. 1, 2 vols. (Henry Holt, 1890), 310.

Skill 18: Fuel Your Fulfillment

1. Mary Oliver, "The Summer Day," *The Truro Bear and Other Adventures: Poems and Essays* (Beacon Press, 2008), 65.
2. Victor H. Vroom, *Work and Motivation* (Wiley, 1964), 17–18.
3. Aristotle, *The Nicomachean Ethics*, trans. W. D. Ross, eds. J. L. Ackrill and J. O. Urmson (Oxford University Press, 2009), bk. 1, chaps. 4–5.
4. Homer, *The Odyssey*, trans. Emily Wilson (W. W. Norton, 2018), 75.
5. "Vocab Insight: Teleios / Whole," BibleProject, accessed September 15, 2025, https://bibleproject.com/videos/vocab-insight-teleios-whole/.
6. Isaiah 10:27; Matthew 11:28–30; John 15:4.
7. Galatians 6:2.
8. Philippians 1:6.

Moving Forward

1. Joshua 3:1–17.
2. Exodus 14:21–22.
3. Joshua 3:8.
4. C. R. Snyder, *The Psychology of Hope: You Can Get There from Here* (Free Press, 1994), 10.

ACKNOWLEDGMENTS

To the many experts whose research formed a solid foundation for this work: Dr. Richard Swenson, Barbara Fredrickson, Mihaly Csikszentmihalyi, Angela Duckworth, Kelly McGonigal, Jim Loehr, and Tony Schwartz.

To my editorial team: My gratitude for the guidance and support of Karissa Taylor, who helped shape this manuscript into its final form, along with the talented team of editors who supported the development of this book, including Kara Mannix, Jocelyn Bailey, Amy Kerr, Jodi Hughes, and Kristen Parrish. To the rest of the team at HarperCollins Christian Publishing, including Stephanie Newton, Denise Froelich, Mandy Wilson, and Chasity Collins, your dedication and talent are truly appreciated.

To my literary champions: I am deeply grateful for the ongoing support of my literary agent, Cynthia Ruchti, and the team at Books & Such Literary Management, who believed in this project and continue to shape me into a better author.

To my mentors and friends: Thank you for your encouragement (and patience) during the long hours of writing, as well as your honest feedback. There are so many individuals who have invested in my development, especially Bill and Patty Schwartz,

Tamara Miranda, Michael and Debbie Scheid, Helen (Lena) and Alexander (Sandy) Astin, Sara Thompson, and Katie McCleary.

To my best friend and biggest champion, Joel. You have served as a sounding board for every idea and concept shared in this book. Thank you for making me countless cups of coffee and folding the bottomless pile of laundry so I could write and edit for hours. I love and admire you!

To our children, Caleb, Luke, and Eden. You remind me daily of the importance of practicing what you teach. I hope this book continues to serve as a resource for you and your children for generations to come!

To you, dear readers, for all the deep work you will do as you practice the skills you've learned. May you continue creating your daily legacies as you enhance your emotional endurance.

And most importantly, to our great God, who designed us in His image as creators with the ability to persist and overcome with His ever-present support. My prayer is that the message of this book glorifies Your eternal work and blesses the lives of those who read it. Amen.

ABOUT THE AUTHOR

Robin Douglas/Contributor, © *Sacramento Business Journal*

Leslie M. Bosserman, M.Ed., CPCC, is an executive coach and lifestyle strategist for innovators and creative professionals leading dynamic and diverse teams. After working for a decade in higher education, Leslie launched Lead With Intention®, a boutique coaching and consulting practice that specializes in leadership development, customized training, and organizational strategy for clients and their teams around the world. She collaborates with a range of creative professionals, from entrepreneurs launching their startups to executive leaders at Fortune 500 companies.

As a two-time UCLA alumna, Leslie graduated with her bachelor's in mass communications and a master's of education. She is also trained as a Certified Professional Co-Active Coach (CPCC) through the Co-Active Training Institute. Leslie currently teaches business and leadership at the University of California, Davis Continuing and Professional Education.

Leslie has been a featured speaker at TEDxEustis, and her talk has drawn over 1.3 million views online. She has also served locally on the leadership team for TEDxSacramento as the event coordinator and volunteered as a coach for emerging female leaders through the Women's Impact Alliance.

Her commitment to enhancing the local community led Leslie and her husband to create and cofound The Makers Place™—the greater Sacramento region's first coworking space with onsite childcare. This innovative business model supports parents who need a professional workspace along with flexible caregiving options. Leslie also currently serves as the director and site supervisor of Mini Makers™ Preschool.

Before becoming an entrepreneur, Leslie worked at the University of Illinois Urbana-Champaign, where she taught leadership and diversity classes and ran a campus-wide leadership certificate program. She also has worked professionally in residential life and academic research at UCLA.

Leslie loves to travel and explore new places and has visited over thirty countries, including living abroad in the Middle East for a year, where she volunteered at local schools in Amman, Jordan, with her husband. She is a novice pickleball player and an expert bargain shopper who loves finding great deals and tackling DIY projects. You can often find her enjoying a cup of local coffee paired with a good book or reading out loud to her children.

Leslie lives in Northern California with her husband and three children and travels internationally for coaching, organizational training, and retreat facilitation. Connect with her at LeslieMBosserman.com and on social media @LeadWithIntention.